CRE**A**TIVE
HOMEOWNER® *Home Arts*

THE **COLOR BOOK** OF
Felted Crochet

AMY O'NEILL HOUCK
STINA RAMOS

PHOTOGRAPHY
Damian Sandone and Steven Mays

SENIOR EDITOR Carol Endler Sterbenz
GRAPHIC DESIGNER Kathryn Wityk
EDITORIAL ASSISTANT Nora Grace
PHOTO EDITOR Robyn Poplasky
DIGITAL IMAGING SPECIALIST Frank Dyer
TECHNICAL EDITORS Amy Swenson, Julie Holetz, and Pat Harste
TECHNICAL ARTIST Jennifer Woods
CONTRIBUTING WRITER Carole Buschmann
INDEXER Schroeder Indexing Services
PRINCIPAL PHOTOGRAPHY Damian Sandone
INSTRUCTIONAL PHOTOGRAPHY Steven Mays
PRODUCER OF PHOTOGRAPHY Genevieve A. Sterbenz
PHOTO STYLIST Deirdre Wegner

Creative Homeowner
VICE PRESIDENT AND PUBLISHER Timothy O. Bakke
PRODUCTION DIRECTOR Kimberly H. Vivas
ART DIRECTOR David Geer
MANAGING EDITOR Fran J. Donegan

Current Printing (last digit)
10 9 8 7 6 5 4 3 2 1

The Color Book of Felted Crochet, First Edition
Library of Congress Control Number: 2007932957
ISBN-10: 1-58011-381-8
ISBN-13: 978-1-58011-381-6

Creative Homeowner®
A Division of Federal Marketing Corp.
24 Park Way, Upper Saddle River, NJ
www.creativehomeowner.com

Pages 130 to 169 appeared in a slightly different version in *Crochet Style: Chic and Sexy Accessories,* pages 130 to 169, © 2007 Creative Homeowner.
The photo (far left) on page 4 and the photo on page 18 appeared in *Faux Florals, Easy Arrangements for All Seasons,* page 78 © 2007 Andy Ryan.

DEDICATED TO JAMES, SELMA, AND JAY. YOU MAKE EVERY DAY COLORFUL.
—Amy O'Neill Houck

TO MY CHILDREN SHANE, CHANT, AND CASSANDRA; TO MY HUSBAND, GEORGE, FOR BEING SUPPORTIVE AND FOR UNDERSTANDING MY PASSION FOR YARN; AND TO MY MOTHER, WHO INSPIRED ME.
—Stina Ramos

Introduction

IMAGINE THAT YOU HAVE SPENT DAYS CROCHETING A SWEATER—YOU'VE CHOSEN YOUR YARN CAREFULLY; YOU'VE MADE A SWATCH; AND YOU'VE FOLLOWED THE PATTERN INSTRUCTIONS. THEN YOU THROW YOUR CREATION INTO A WASHING MACHINE FILLED WITH HOT WATER—ON PURPOSE! THIS IS THE KIND OF FUN THAT YOU'LL HAVE WHEN YOU MAKE THE BEAUTIFUL GARMENTS AND ACCESSORIES IN **THE COLOR BOOK OF FELTED CROCHET**. INSPIRED BY THE COLORS OF NATURE, EACH BEAUTIFUL CREATION IS A TIMELESS CLASSIC THAT YOU CAN MAKE USING THE CLEAR AND EASY-TO-FOLLOW DIRECTIONS THAT ACCOMPANY EACH ORIGINAL.

There are 25 designs, including skirts, sweaters, coats, a vest, bags, hats, and mittens—all designed by Stina Ramos and crocheted in a broad range of colors—from muted pastels and **vivid shades** to **natural and neutral tones.**

All of the projects in **The Color Book of Felted Crochet** combine felting, one of the oldest techniques for making fabric, and crochet, one of the most fashion-forward of the needle arts. When most people think of felting, they think of something that is heavy and stiff, but we wanted to bring a new look to felted crochet and make garments—not just bags and hats. There's a range of felting in the book, and some projects combine felted crochet with non-felted crochet accents, resulting in unique designs that have an interesting mix of texture and contemporary style.

To ensure good results, be sure to read "Felting Basics," on pages 162 to 169, before you begin a project. We have included all the step-by-step information and the tips and guides that you will need to become a crocheting and felting pro. When it comes to fit, we encourage you to consider the patterns and schematics as guides, making careful changes according to your own measurements to make sure that the final piece is comfortable to wear. With the instructions and beautiful designs in the book, we've provided a framework from which you can create and explore. Let **The Color Book of Felted Crochet** inspire you!

Stina Ramos

Table of Contents

The Principles of Color and Felting

In creating this book, we combined color theory with felting techniques to create distinct style and beauty in the garments and accessories featured in "the Collection." By mastering a few fundamentals, you will learn to use color to coordinate your felted garments and accessories. The introduction to the world of felted crochet will help you create one-of-a kind pieces that add signature style to your wardrobe.

Color Principles

What makes a garment memorable? What gives a sweater, coat, or skirt that certain "must-have" look? The shape, texture, and hand of a garment play roles in inspiring our preferences, but often it is color that tips the fine balance toward a garment or accessory being chosen and worn. In *The Color Book of Felted Crochet*, color plays a significant role in conveying the mood, silhouette, and style of a particular piece of apparel and the person who wears it.

The collection of garments and accessories featured in this book is divided into three main chapters that concentrate on distinct color groups—muted pastels, bright and vivid shades, and subtle natural and neutral hues. Each distinct color grouping is expressed in an appealing range of projects that shifts across the particular colorway, providing an exciting and stylish set of one-of-a-kind garments and accessories that can be created using felted crochet.

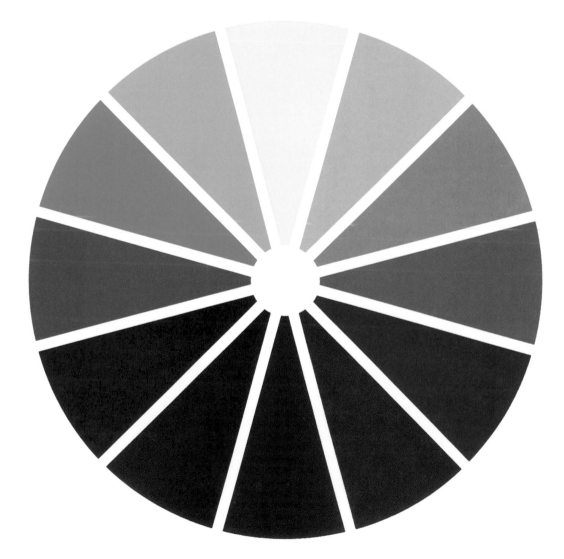

Color is emotional.

Color appeals to us on an emotional level and influences our choices. Color is all around us, and we develop strong preferences for certain colors, choosing them over and over again. Perhaps we identify a particular color as one that flatters our complexion or that plays up our personality. Here, the spirited pink-red fuchsia of the "Amaranth" jacket, left, and the soft, muted-squash color of the long coat "Delicata," right, are wonderful examples of how color can make your heart sing. Who wouldn't want to throw the swingy coat, "Delicata," over a pair of jeans, or combine it with a witty mix of other favorites? Whether light or dark, color can play up our best features and lift our spirits.

Color inspires the imagination.

Picture a golden retriever being taken on a country walk by a chic woman in the contemporary cowl-neck sweater, "Blue-Flower," below. Would you imagine a standard poodle, a slim greyhound, or a small fluffy dog instead if she were wearing the bright-pink "Amaranth" jacket featured on page 9? If "Blue Flower" were made in navy blue or Tuscan orange, would you imagine another coterie of pets? Color communicates our personal tastes and style and can inspire others to associate our preferences with a particular lifestyle.

Color makes objects recede or stand out.

A garment, even one in a pale color, can stand out when paired with a coordinate in a hot color. Warm colors (those with a yellow undertone) and primary colors tend to move forward, attracting the viewer's attention. The feminine shrug, "Picot Fan," top, is worn with a bright-orange cami, making it the center of attraction. The strong contrast between the cami and the shrug highlights the delicate filigree of stitches on the shrug. When the "Picot-Fan" shrug is worn with a medium-gray dress, bottom, the low-contrast ensemble appears to recede.

Color defines shape and form.

Pastel and neutral colors tend to create silhouettes that are more subtle than those generated by bright colors, which make the contour of any garment or accessory more noticeable. Look at the way the dynamic tropical color of "Coral Reef," below, dramatizes the geometric shape of the sweater and highlights the decorative stitch used to make the crocheted fabric. Dark colors, such as brown, navy, and black, are noted for accentuating the shape of garments and accessories. The "Peony" tote shown on page 14 is made in a rich black that delineates the bag's silhouette and provides a bold backdrop for the graphic-style flower in creamy white.

Color communicates style.

The burgundy red of the skirt, "Wine and Roses," right, has sophisticated style—its simple lines give the skirt a vintage feel and trace the shape of the body, showing off its subtle curves. The multicolored roses that are added as a separate, tasteful decoration attract the eye to the hip area of the skirt. Had the skirt been made in burnt orange and the corsage of roses in purple, the style of the skirt would be more funky and contemporary. To decide on your personal style, renew your understanding of the color wheel on page 8 so that you can work more effectively with related or contrasting colors. Notice how the primary, secondary, and tertiary colors flow, blend, and contrast with one another. You will be able to use those principles to come up with new color combinations that appeal to your personality and to choose colors that please and flatter you.

Felting Principles

If you were one of those kids who loved chemistry lab or if you're a baker who likes watching dough become bread in the oven, you'll love felting—it's got that same "magic." In felted crochet, fiber is transformed from strand into mass—stitches lose definition; fabric shrinks; and soft and flexible become sturdy and thick.

When you felt, you're participating in an ancient technique. Historians speculate that felting was a lucky accident. Imagine someone wrapping wool fleece around her feet for warmth. After walking in the wool wraps for days, she discovers that the original wads of fleece have changed into contoured booties that are strong, snug, and resistant to cold and moisture.

What is felting?

Felting happens when yarn made of animal fiber is subjected to heat, moisture, and friction, transforming the individual hairs into a solid mass. Technically speaking, all of the "felting" in this book is actually "fulling," which is a term used to describe the process of felting animal fiber that has aleady been crocheted, knit-ted, or woven into fabric.

Why do animal fibers felt?

Try this: hold a strand of your own hair, and slide your fin-gers down along the shaft from your scalp to the tip; then slide your fingers upward. You'll notice that the strand feels much smoother when your fingers slide down the hair than when they slide up. The sub-tle roughness that you feel on the upward stroke is the hair's scales that cover the strand in a pattern that resembles shingles on a roof. When yarn made of ani-mal hair is subjected to the felting process, these scales open up and interlock with one another, pro-ducing felted fabric.

What yarns are "feltable"?

Only yarns made from animal fibers will felt. Yarn made from sheep's wool is most commonly used in felting, but other animal fibers, such as cashmere and llama, will felt, too. Every animal fiber felts a little differently—yarn made from alpaca shrinks a lot, while wool blends need more processing to make them felt. Make sure that your yarn is at least 50 percent animal fiber. When you are buying yarn for felting, pay close attention to the label. Listed is specific informa-tion about the yarn's fiber con-tent that will indicate whether the yarn will felt or not. Look for a label that says "hand wash" or "dry clean only." Those labeled "superwash" and "washable" will not felt. If you are combining two different color yarns in a project, be aware that dye and bleaching processes can affect the quality of the felting and cause the yarns to felt in different ways. Ask for advice about particular yarn choices at your yarn shop.

Should I make a test swatch?

Always make a test swatch because every felting process is different. Crochet a 10-inch-square swatch, and test-felt it before you begin your project. If your project is done "in the round," make your swatch in the round. Be sure your gauge matches the before-felting (B/F) gauge specified in the pattern. Remember that felting is chemistry. The type of yarn, the temperature and hardness of the water, the kind of soap, and the amount of agitation affect the felting outcome. By making a swatch, you'll learn how to adjust certain variables, especially soaking time and agitation. Use the fill-in tables on pages 170 to 171 to keep track of your felting trials. *Note: even if you're using the yarn that is specified in the project, your result might be slightly different from those shown.*

Which measurements do I use?

Before you begin to crochet your garment, decide which **finished size** listed in the pattern is best suited to your body measurements. Refer to the "finished size" section at the beginning of the materials list in each project for a range of sizes from x-small to x-large. The finished size represents the measurements of the *completed* garment after it has been felted, blocked, and assembled and includes any edgings, seams, and non-felted details. For example, the finished size of the "Delicata" coat, right, includes the ruffled edging and the crocheted strips along the sleeves.

When you are ready to begin work, use the **before-felting (B/F)** measurements noted on the *schematic diagram*, left, to crochet the individual piece(s). The before-felting (B/F) measurements are larger than the **after-felting (A/F)** measurements, indicating the amount of shrinkage that occurs during the felting process.

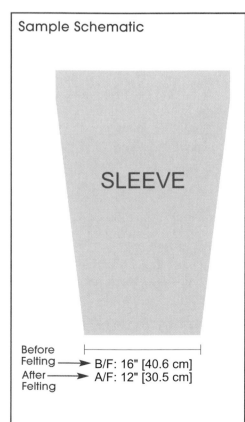

Sample Schematic

SLEEVE

| Before Felting | → | B/F: 16" [40.6 cm] |
| After Felting | → | A/F: 12" [30.5 cm] |

Size Information

To choose a garment size that fits you, look at the "Finished Size" section that begins the materials list for each project in "The Collection."

finished size*

(*completed coat after felting, blocking, assembling, and finishing)

- **X-Small:** 38" (96.5cm) bust and 34" (86.4cm) long
- **Small:** 40" (101.6cm) bust and 34" (86.4cm) long
- **Medium:** 44" (111.8cm) bust and 35½" (90.2cm) long
- **Large:** 48" (121.9cm) bust and 37½" (95.3cm) long
- **X-Large:** 52" (132.1cm) bust and 37½" (95.3cm) long

felting principles (cont'd.)

Soft-Felting and Hard-Felting

Soft-felting changes the crocheted fabric slightly, creating a "blurred" pattern that keeps some of its stitch definition. A soft-felted fabric remains pliable and soft, and is the preferred texture for most felted garments.

Hard-felting shrinks the crocheted fabric to its maximum, resulting in a fabric that is sturdy and thick without stitch definition. A fabric that is hard-felted is suited to bags, totes, and hats. Because hard-felted fabric does not ravel, it can be cut with scissors.

Soft-Felting

Hard-Felting

Gauge

Stitch gauge is extremely important in crochet, especially if you are felting your crocheted fabric, which will cause the fabric to shrink and the stitches to pack together. You will notice that each pattern makes a note of the gauge before-felting (B/F) the project and after-felting (A/F) it. You might feel that you're working your stitches too loosely, but the looser gauge is designed to provide room for the stitches to rub against one another and for the fabric to shrink.

Before Felting

After Felting

felting equipment, materials, and tools

HARDWARE

- **Washing Machine.** All of the projects in this book are machine felted. Make sure that you know how to stop your machine mid-cycle so that you can check your project. (With a top-loading washer, you may only need to lift the lid or pull out the power button to stop agitation.) While your garment is agitating, check it every minute. You can use a timer, but standing nearby is best. Felting can happen very quickly. If you're using a front-loading washer, check your project less frequently, perhaps every 10 to 15 minutes. Front loaders felt slowly and need to be drained each time you check your work.

- **Lingerie Bag or Zippered Pillow Case.** Felting causes fibers to be released from the crocheted fabric. A mesh bag will contain these, preventing them from clogging the machine. If your washing machine drains into a utility sink, attach a mesh sieve to the end of the drain hose. These inexpensive metal "socks" slip over the end of the hose and are secured with a zip tie.

- **Towels.** When I was a kid, my mom would wash all of our sweaters by hand and then roll each of them in a towel to remove the excess water. She did this to save the garments from being stretched and pulled out of shape—the result if wrung by hand or allowed to go through the machine's spin cycle.

- **Optional: Portable Dryer.** This handy dryer has a layer of mesh fabric stretched over its metal frame, allowing garments to dry flat and air to circulate.

- **Blocking Aids.** Use a hard form to block and to maintain the shape of your crocheted items as they dry, especially structured hats and bags. While your head (if you can endure it) works well for blocking hats, you can also use a plastic bowl or other kitchen item that has the same measurements as your project. First work the project with your hands, stretching it until it takes the correct shape. Then use your blocking aid, allowing the project to dry completely before removing it.

- **Hot Water.** The *exact* temperature of hot water used to felt fabric is not important—hot water from the tap will felt—but temperature will affect the *rate* of felting. In general, the hotter the water, the faster the fabric will felt. If desired, keep track of the water temperature, using an oven or a candy thermometer.

- **Plastic Container.** Use a big, clean bucket or plastic container to felt small projects, such as mittens and scarves, by hand. Put on rubber gloves, and use your hands to agitate the project. You will find that hand-felting provides more control over the rate of felting because you are more closely involved in the process.

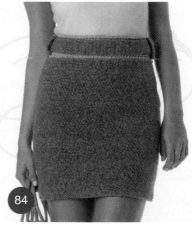

30

34

40

44

64

68

71

72

94

100

122

126

DISCOVER THE GORGEOUS NEW SILHOU-ETTES, STYLISH LOOKS, AND APPEALING COLORWAYS OF THE BEAUTIFUL GAR-MENTS AND ACCESSORIES FEATURED IN **THE COLOR BOOK OF FELTED CROCHET.** CREATED BY COMBINING TWO UNIQUE CRAFTS, CROCHET AND FELTING, EACH ORIGINAL DESIGN—FROM SKIRTS, VESTS, SWEATERS, SHRUGS, AND CAPELETS TO SCARVES, MITTENS, BAGS, AND HATS—IS FLATTERING AND SEXY, AND PERFECT FOR ANY OCCASION.

Muted Pastels

Subtle and seductive, the pastel tones of the projects in this chapter draw you in. They make you want to look closer. They can be soothing and cheerful; they can stir memories of childhood or evoke fantasies of a tropical paradise. Pastel colorways are lighter, softer versions of their vivid cousins—pink is the temperate version of red's passion; sky blue is a relaxing version of the high energy of bright blue.

Muted pastels play out in such garments as "Delicata," a long coat in autumn's garden-inspired squash color, and in the subtle tones of "Allotrope," a fitted, smoky-charcoal U-neck vest that is a perfect layering piece over almost any other color. A pale-pink wash of color defines "Fairy Floss," a sweater with dramatic styling. Variegated pink, strawberry, cream, and chocolate mix together in the "Andean" mittens and scarf, an ensemble that will add playful elegance to your winter wardrobe. In "Blue Flower," subtle variations of blue evoke a field of wildflowers in a slightly fitted, cowl-neck sweater, and eggshell blue makes an appearance in "Picot Fan," a shrug with antique-lace details. Two hats add great style to this chapter— "Fedora," a jaunty hat in hazy purple reminiscent of those worn in old movies, and "Siberian Jewel," a fez-style toque in an amethyst-colored mohair that has the look and feel of real fur.

Blue Flower

THE COLOR BLUE IS SO RARELY FOUND IN NATURE THAT IT IS ASSOCIATED WITH THE "UNOBTAINABLE"—BUT NOT ANY MORE. HERE, A SLATE-BLUE YARN IS USED TO MAKE "BLUE FLOWER," A TUNIC-LENGTH SWEATER WITH A DEEP U-NECK AND SHAWL COLLAR. MADE FROM BABY-ALPACA YARN, THIS SWEATER ALLOWS YOU STYLISH FLEXIBILTY. YOU CAN WEAR THE ULTRA-WARM TOP WITHOUT OVERHEATING. THROWN OVER JEANS OR LEGGINGS AND A T-SHIRT, "BLUE FLOWER" IS THE ULTIMATE IN LAST-MINUTE GLAMOUR.

skill level

Intermediate

finished size*

*(completed sweater after felting, blocking, assembling, and finishing)
- **Small/Medium:** 40" (101.6cm) bust and 25" (63.5cm) long
- **Large/X-Large:** 46" (116.8cm) bust and 25" (63.5cm) long

before-felting (B/F) and after-felting (A/F) measurements

See schematic.

materials

- Blue Sky Alpacas Melange: 100% baby alpaca (110 yds. (100.5m) / 1¾ oz. (50g)), color #800 cornflower, 18 (22) skeins

notions

- Tapestry needle

hooks

- K/10½ (6.50mm), or size needed to obtain gauge
- G/6 (4.00mm), or size needed to obtain gauge

gauge

- 12 hdc and 10 rows = 4" (10.2cm) with larger hook in Rib pat st before felting
- 12 hdc = 3" (7.6cm) and 10 rows = 3⅜" (8.6cm) with larger hook in Rib pat st after felting

notes

- Each piece is made vertically, side edge to side edge.
- Back, front, and sleeves are felted; cowl collar is not.
- Turning chain does not count as stitch.

abbreviations

See page 141.

Before Felting

After Felting

Blue Flower

SPECIAL ABBREVIATIONS
Shell: Work 5 dc in same st.
Dc2tog: (Yo, insert hook into st, yo and pull up loop, yo and pull through 2 loops on hook) twice, yo and pull through all 3 loops on hook.
Dc5tog: (Yo, insert hook into st, yo and pull up loop, yo and pull through 2 loops on hook) 5 times, yo and pull through all 6 loops on hook.

SPECIAL STITCHES
Rib Pattern Stitch (Rib pat st)
Row 1: Ch 2, hdc in each st across, turn.
Row 2: Ch 2, working in back loops only, hdc in each st across, turn.
Rows 3–5: Ch 2, working in front loops only, hdc in each st across, turn.
Row 6: Rep Row 2.
Rep Rows 1–6 for Rib pat st.

Shell Pattern Stitch (Shell pat st)
(Multiple of 4 sts plus 1)
Row 1: Ch 5, skip first 2 sts, * work Shell in next st, skip next 3 sts; rep from * across to last 2 sts, dc in top of tch, turn.
Row 2: Ch 1, sc in each st across, turn.
Row 3: Ch 3, skip first 2 sts, * work dc5tog over next Shell, ch 3; rep from * to last st, end dc in last sc.
Work Rows 1–3 for Shell pat st.

SWEATER
BACK
Beg at side edge, ch 101 loosely.
Foundation Row: Hdc in 3rd ch from hook and in each ch across, turn (99 hdc).
Work in Rib pat st until 59 (67) rows have been com-pleted from beg; piece should measure approx. 24 (27)" (61.0 (68.6)cm). Fasten off.

FRONT
Work as for Back until 10 (14) rows have been completed from beg; the piece should measure approx. 4 (5½)" (10.2 (14.0)cm).

RIGHT NECK SHAPING
Row 1 (RS): Ch 2, work in Rib pat st across first 50 sts, hdc2tog, turn leaving rem 47 sts unworked (51 hdc).
Row 2: Ch 2, work in Rib pat st in each st across, turn.
Row 3: Ch 2, work in Rib pat st to last 2 sts, hdc2tog, turn (50 hdc). Rep Rows 2 and 3 seven times more (43 hdc). Work even until 34 (38) rows have been finished.

LEFT NECK SHAPING
Row 1 (RS): Ch 2, work in Rib pat st to last st, work 2 hdc in last st, turn (44 hdc).
Row 2: Ch 2, work in Rib pat st in each st across, turn. Rep Rows 1 and 2 six times more, then rep Row 1 once; do not turn (51 hdc).

Next Row (WS): Ch 49, turn, hdc in third ch from hook and in next 46 ch, work in Rib pat st to end, turn (99 hdc). Work even for 9 (13) rows more; 59 (67) rows have been completed from beg, and Front should be approximately same width as Back. Fasten off.

SLEEVES (Make 2.)
Ch 63 loosely.
Foundation Row: Hdc in third ch from hook and in each ch across, turn (61 hdc).
Cont in Rib pat st until piece measures 9½" (24.1cm) from beg.
Work Rows 1–3 of Shell pat st.
Cont in Rib pat st until piece measures 19" (48.3cm) from beg. Fasten off. Weave in all loose ends.

FELTING
See "Felting Basics" on pages 160 to 169. Check and measure your sweater frequently during the felting process. Felt and block to the after-felting (A/F) measurements listed in the schematic, and lay the sweater flat to dry.

ASSEMBLING
Sew shoulder seams. Sew on Sleeves, centering Shell pat st with shoulder seams. Sew side and sleeve seams.

COLLAR (Not Felted)
Ch 31 loosely.
Foundation Row: Hdc in third ch from hook and in each ch across, turn (29 hdc).
Cont in Rib pat st until piece measures 52" (132.1cm) from beg. Fasten off.
Sew short edges of Collar together. With ribbed side of neckband facing to RS, sew one long edge of neckband to neck edge, placing seam at center back neck edge, stretching Collar slightly to fit.

COLLAR EDGING (Not Felted)
With RS of Collar facing, join yarn with sl st at center back edge.
Rnd 1: Ch 1, working from left to right, reverse sc evenly around edge, join rnd with sl st in first st. Fasten off.

FINISHING
Weave in all remaining loose ends.

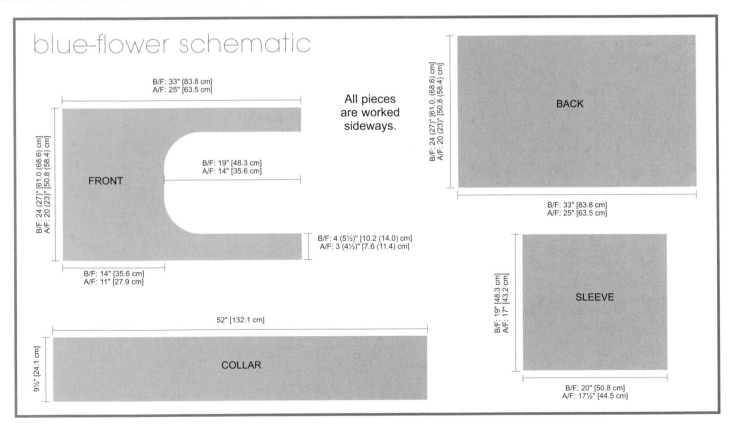

blue-flower schematic

All pieces are worked sideways.

FRONT
B/F: 33" [83.8 cm]
A/F: 25" [63.5 cm]
B/F: 19" [48.3 cm]
A/F: 14" [35.6 cm]
B/F: 24 (27)" [61.0 (68.6) cm]
A/F: 20 (23)" [50.8 (58.4) cm]
B/F: 4 (5½)" [10.2 (14.0) cm]
A/F: 3 (4½)" [7.6 (11.4) cm]
B/F: 14" [35.6 cm]
A/F: 11" [27.9 cm]

BACK
B/F: 24 (27)" [61.0 (68.6) cm]
A/F: 20 (23)" [50.8 (58.4) cm]
B/F: 33" [83.8 cm]
A/F: 25" [63.5 cm]

SLEEVE
B/F: 19" [48.3 cm]
A/F: 17" [43.2 cm]
B/F: 20" [50.8 cm]
A/F: 17½" [44.5 cm]

COLLAR
52" [132.1 cm]
9½" [24.1 cm]

Fairy Floss

A LIGHT FLUFF OF PINK SWEETNESS, "FAIRY FLOSS" IS A YOUTHFUL INDULGENCE OF "SUGAR" SPUN INTO FINE THREAD. IN THIS SWEATER, FINE ALPACA AND ANGORA FIBERS ARE BLENDED TOGETHER TO CREATE A LIGHT AND SUPER-SOFT FABRIC WITH INCREDIBLE WARMTH. THIS EASY-TO-CROCHET SWEATER IS CREATED FROM SIMPLE SHAPES. THE DRAMATIC DOLMAN SLEEVES AND LACE-SEAM DETAILING ADD RUNWAY STYLE TO THE COZY, COMFORTABLE SWEATER THAT'S SURE TO BECOME A FAVORITE IN YOUR WARDROBE.

Before Felting

After Felting

skill level

Intermediate

finished size*

(*completed sweater after felting, blocking, assembling, and finishing)
- **Small/Medium:** 32"–38" (81.3cm–96.5cm) bust
- **Large/X-Large:** 40"–44" (101.6cm–111.8cm) bust

before-felting (B/F) and after-felting (A/F) measurements

See schematic.

materials

- Cascade Yarns Indulgence: 70% superfine alpaca, 30% wool (123 yds. (112.5m)/ 1¾ oz. (50g)), color #528, 10 (12) skeins

notions

- Tapestry needle

hooks

- I/9 (5.50mm), or size needed to obtain gauge
- G/6 (4.00mm), or size needed to obtain gauge

gauge

- 12 hdc and 10 rows = 4" (10.2cm) before felting
- 12 hdc = 3¼" (8.2cm) and 10 rows = 3½" (8.9cm) after felting

notes

- Back, front, and sleeves are four identical pieces.
- Back, front, and sleeves are soft-felted.
- Seam details, edgings, and ribbed bands are not felted.
- Turning chain does not count as hdc unless indicated.

abbreviations

See page 141.

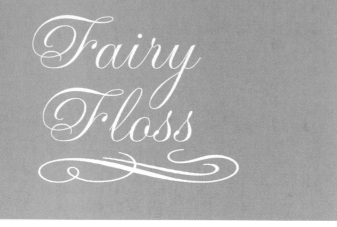

Fairy Floss

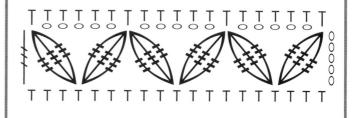

SPECIAL ABBREVIATION

Dtr Bobble: In same st, (yo 3 times, insert hook into st, yo and pull up a loop, (yo and pull through 2 loops on hook) 3 times, yo and pull through all 4 loops on hook.

SPECIAL STITCH

Leaf Bar Stitch (Leaf Bar st)
(Multiple of 6 sts)
Row 1 (WS): Ch 2, hdc in each st across, turn.
Row 2: Ch 5 (counts as 1 dtr), skip next 3 sts, work (Dtr Bobble, ch 5, Dtr Bobble) all in next st, * skip next 5 sts, work (Dtr Bobble, ch 5, Dtr Bobble) all in next st; rep from * to last 3 sts, skip next 2 sts, dtr in last st, turn.
Row 3: Ch 1, hdc in each st and work 5 hdc in each ch-5 sp across, end hdc in top of ch-5 tch.
Work Rows 1–3 for Leaf Bar st.

SWEATER
BACK, FRONT, AND SLEEVES
(Make 4.)
Work from the neck to the bottom edge.
With larger hook, ch 37.
Row 1: Hdc in third ch from hook and in each ch across, turn (35 hdc).

For Size Small/Medium
Row 2: Ch 2, working through front loops only, hdc in each st across, turn.
Row 3: Ch 2, work 2 hdc in first st, hdc in each st to last st, work 2 hdc in last st, turn (37 hdc).
Rep Rows 2 and 3 until piece measures approx. 20½" (52.1cm) from beg.

For Size Large/Extra Large
Row 2: Ch 2, working through front loops only, work

2 hdc in first st, hdc in each st to last st, work 2 hdc in last st, turn (37 hdc)
Row 3: Ch 2, work 2 hdc in first st, hdc in each st to last st, work 2 hdc in last st, turn (39 hdc).
Rep Rows 2 and 3 twice more (47 hdc).
Row 4: Ch 2, working through front loops only, hdc in each st across, turn.
Row 5: Ch 2, work 2 hdc in first st, hdc in each st to last st, work 2 hdc in last st, turn (49 hdc).
Rep Rows 4 and 5 until piece measures 23½" (59.7cm) from beg.

FINISHING
Weave in all loose ends.

FELTING
See "Felting Basics" on pages 160 to169. Check and measure your sweater frequently during the felting process. Felt and block the sweater to the after-felting (A/F) measurements listed in the schematic, and lay it flat to dry.

SLEEVE SEAM DETAIL (Not Felted)
With RS facing and smaller hook, join yarn with sl st in bottom side edge of one sleeve piece.
Foundation Row (RS): Ch 1, work 108 (120) sc evenly spaced along side edge, turn. Work Rows 1–3 of Leaf Bar st. Fasten off. With RS facing and smaller hook, join yarn with sl st in top side edge of same piece. Rep Foundation Row, then Rows 1–3 of Leaf Bar st. Fasten off. Rep for second sleeve.

BACK SIDE EDGING (Not Felted)
With RS facing and smaller hook, join yarn with sl st in bottom side edge of one piece.

Foundation Row (RS): Ch 1, work 108 (120) sc evenly spaced along side edge. Fasten off.
With RS facing and smaller hook, join yarn with sl st in top side edge of same piece. Rep foundation row. Fasten off.

FRONT SIDE EDGING (Not Felted)
Work as for back side edging.

ASSEMBLING
Sew the side edges of the Sleeves to the Front and Back pieces. At the bottom edge of each Sleeve, sew the side edges of the Leaf Bar st together to close the Sleeve.

SLEEVE EDGING (Not Felted)
With RS facing and smaller hook, join yarn with sl st in underarm seam.
Rnd 1: Ch 1, sc evenly around entire bottom edge, join rnd with sl st in first st. Fasten off.

(continued on page 28)

HELPFUL TIP

If you are felting an item in the washing machine, especially small crocheted projects, put in other items such as a pair of jeans or a heavy sweatshirt to add friction and help the felting process along.

fairy-floss schematic

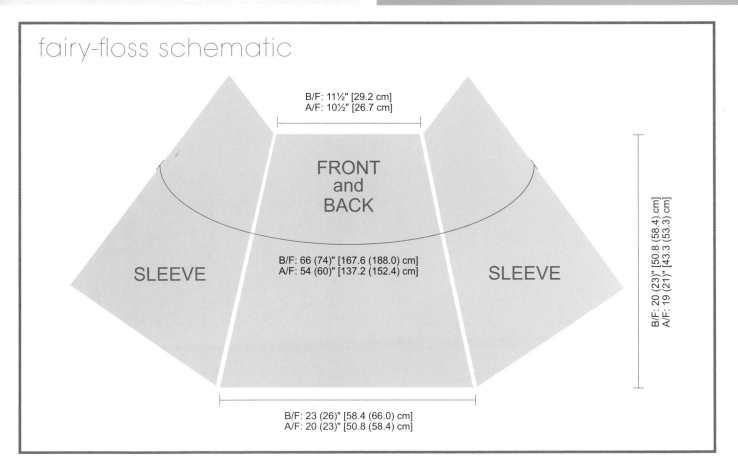

B/F: 11½" [29.2 cm]
A/F: 10½" [26.7 cm]

FRONT
and
BACK

SLEEVE

B/F: 66 (74)" [167.6 (188.0) cm]
A/F: 54 (60)" [137.2 (152.4) cm]

SLEEVE

B/F: 20 (23)" [50.8 (58.4) cm]
A/F: 19 (21)" [43.3 (53.3) cm]

B/F: 23 (26)" [58.4 (66.0) cm]
A/F: 20 (23)" [50.8 (58.4) cm]

Fairy Floss

(continued from page 27)

RIBBED NECKBAND (Not Felted)
With smaller hook, ch 17.
Row 1: Hdc in third ch from hook and in each ch across, turn (15 hdc).
Row 2: Ch 2, working in back loops only, hdc in each st across, turn.
Rep Row 2 until piece measures 30 (34)" (76.2 (86.4)cm) from beg (unstretched). Fasten off.

Sew short edges of Neckband together.
With ribbed side of Neckband facing to RS, sew one long edge of Neckband to neck edge, placing seam at center back neck, and stretching Neckband to fit.

RIBBED BOTTOM BAND (Not Felted)
With smaller hook, ch 32.
Row 1: Hdc in third ch from hook and in each ch across, turn (30 hdc).
Row 2: Ch 2, working in back loops only, hdc in each st across, turn.
Rep Row 2 until piece measures 34 (38)" (86.4 (96.5)cm) from beg (unstretched). Fasten off.

Sew short edges of Bottom Band together.
With ribbed side of Bottom Band facing to RS, sew one long edge of Bottom Band to bottom edge, placing seam at center back and stretching Bottom Band to fit.

Weave in all remaining loose ends.

…yet cozy

Traditional dolman sleeves are very wide at the armholes and narrow at the wrists, but in "Fairy Floss," the dolman sleeves end at the wrists in wide billows that add drama and a modern sensibility to the sweater. Defined by pretty bands of filigree lace, the cape~style sleeves show off the flat~tering band at the waist.

Fedora

While the fedora is an icon of vintage menswear and a favorite of *film-noir* stars, it originated as a woman's hat. Our hat is named after the French play *Fédora* in which the heroine, Princess Fedora Romazova, sported the style. *Fédora* was written for and first performed by Sarah Bernhardt. Her immense popularity made the hat an immediate fashion hit. This fedora is hard-felted in smooth Merino wool and embellished with narrow bands of leather.

Before Felting

After Felting

skill level

Elementary

finished size*

(*completed hat after felting and blocking)
- 22" (55.9cm) circumference and 6¼" (15.9cm) from crown to brim; fits an average woman's head

before-felting (B/F) measurements

- 29½" (74.9cm) circumference
- 8" (20.3cm) height, from brim to top of crown
- 4" (10.2cm) width of brim

materials

- Vermont Organics O-Wool: 100% organic Merino wool (198 yds. (178.2m) / 3½ oz. (100g)), color cornflower, 2 skeins

notions

- Tapestry needle
- Bowl (for mold)
- 1¼ yd. (1.1m) leather trim in width as desired (for hat band and edge of brim)
- Permanent fabric glue

hook

- I/9 (5.50mm), or size needed to obtain gauge

gauge

- 10 hdc and 8 rows = 4" (10.2cm) before felting
- 10 hdc and 8 rows = 3" (7.6cm) after felting

notes

- Hat is crocheted, then felted and blocked.
- Turning chain does not count as stitch.

abbreviations

See page 141.

Fedora

HAT
Ch 17.

CROWN
Rnd 1: Work 2 hdc in third ch from hook, hdc in next 13 ch, work 4 hdc in last ch, turn to work in bottom loops of foundation ch, hdc in next 13 loops, work 2 hdc in next loop, join rnd with a sl st in first st (34 hdc).
Rnd 2: Ch 2, work 2 hdc in each of next 2 sts, hdc in next 13 sts, work 2 hdc in each of next 4 sts, hdc in next 13 sts, work 2 hdc in each of last 2 sts, join rnd with sl st in first st (42 hdc).
Rnd 3: Ch 2, hdc in first 2 sts, work 2 hdc in each of next 2 sts, hdc in next 15 sts, work 2 hdc in each of next 2 sts, hdc in next 2 sts, work 2 hdc in each of next 2 sts, hdc in next 15 sts, work 2 hdc in each of last 2 sts, join rnd with sl st in first st (50 hdc).

Rnd 4: Ch 2, hdc in first 3 sts, work 2 hdc in each of next 2 sts, hdc in next 18 sts, work 2 hdc in each of next 2 sts, hdc in next 3 sts, work 2 hdc in each of next 2 sts, hdc in next 18 sts, work 2 hdc in each of last 2 sts, join rnd with sl st in first st (58 hdc).
Rnd 5: Ch 2, hdc in first 4 sts, work 2 hdc in each of next 2 sts, hdc in next 21 sts, work 2 hdc in each of next 2 sts, hdc in next 4 sts, work 2 hdc in each of next 2 sts, hdc in next 21 sts, work 2 hdc in last 2 sts, join rnd with sl st in first st (66 hdc).
Rnd 6: Ch 2, hdc in first 5 sts, work 2 hdc in each of next 2 sts, hdc in next 24 sts, work 2 hdc in each of next 2 sts, hdc in next 5 sts, work 2 hdc in each of next 2 sts, hdc in next 24 sts, work 2 hdc in each of last 2 sts, join rnd with sl st in first st (74 hdc).
Rnd 7: Ch 2, working in back loops only, hdc in each st around, join rnd with sl st in first st.
Rnds 8–22: Ch 2, hdc in each st around, join rnd with sl st in first st.

BRIM
Rnd 23: Ch 2, * hdc in next 2 sts, work 2 hdc in next st; rep from * around, end hdc in last 2 sts, join rnd with sl st in first st (98 hdc).
Rnd 24: Ch 2, hdc in each st around, join rnd with sl st in first st.
Rnd 25: Ch 2, * hdc in next 3 sts, work 2 hdc in next st; rep from * around, end hdc in last 2 sts, join rnd with sl

A crocheted hat is a perfect felting project for a beginner. Because this hat is worked in one piece using simple stitches, you can explore such techniques as making increases, creating a flat circle, and working in rounds. You needn't worry about mistakes~they'll be hidden in this hard~felted project.

HELPFUL TIP

Spice up your "Fedora" with easy
embellishments. Change the hatband from
leather to a pretty ribbon, or sew on a feather.
You can create a feather from felted
scraps left over from other projects
and add it to your hat.

st in first st (122 hdc).
Rnd 26: Rep Rnd 24.
Rnd 27: Ch 2, * hdc in next 4 sts, work 2 hdc in next st;
rep from * around, end hdc in last 2 sts, join rnd with sl
st in first st (146 hdc).
Rnd 28: Rep Rnd 24.
Rnd 29: Ch 2, * hdc in next 5 sts, work 2 hdc in next st;
rep from * around, end hdc in last 2 sts, join rnd with sl
st in first st (170 hdc).
Rnd 30: Rep Rnd 24. Fasten off.

FINISHING
Weave in all loose ends.

FELTING
See "Felting Basics" on pages 160 to 169. The hat is
hard-felted. Felt the hat, checking it for fit during the
felting process. **Note:** the hat should fit snugly on the
crown of your head. Block the hat over a bowl or container, shaping it as desired. Let the hat dry thoroughly.

EMBELLISHING
Cut two lengths of trim: one equal to the circumference of the crown at the beginning of the brim plus
1/2" (1.3cm); and the second equal to the circumference of the edge of the brim plus 1/2" (1.3cm). Glue
the trim as shown in the photograph, abutting the ends
and trimming off the excess.

Delicata

THE SQUASH BEGINS LIFE AS A DELICATE YEL-LOW-ORANGE FLOWER WITH A SOFT, RUFFLED EDGE THAT UNCURLS AS IT GROWS TO ITS FULL, SHOWY BLOOM. HERE, "DELICATA," A PRETTY COAT IN A SIMILAR HUE, IS ACCENTED WITH A WIDE BAND OF INTRICATE LACE. THE SLIM CUT AND ELBOW-LENGTH SLEEVES GIVE THE GAR-MENT A MODERN SILHOUETTE. "DELICATA" CAN BE WORN OVER A DRESS FOR A NIGHT OUT OR WITH A PAIR OF JEANS ON A CRISP FALL DAY. THE MODIFIED DROP-SHOULDER CONSTRUC-TION MAKES "DELICATA" A BREEZE TO CROCHET.

Before Felting

After Felting

skill level

Advanced

finished size*

(*completed coat after felting, blocking, assembling, and finishing)
- **X-Small:** 38" (96.5cm) bust and 33" (83.8cm) long
- **Small:** 40" (101.6cm) bust and 33" (83.8cm) long
- **Medium:** 44" (111.8cm) bust and 35" (88.9cm) long
- **Large:** 48" (121.9cm) bust and 37" (94.0cm) long
- **X-Large:** 52" (132.1cm) bust and 37" (94.0cm) long

before-felting (B/F) and after-felting (A/F) measurements

See schematic.

materials

- Cascade Yarns 220 Heather: 100% Peruvian highland wool (220 yds. (201.2m) / 3½ oz. (100g)), color #2437, 13 (14, 15, 16, 17) skeins

notions

- Tapestry needle

hook

- I/9 (5.50mm), or size needed to obtain gauge

gauge

- 11 hdc and 9 rows = 4" (10.2cm) before felting
- 11 hdc = 2¾" (7.0cm) and 9 rows = 3½" (8.9cm) after felting

notes

- Back, fronts, and sleeves are felted.
- Collar, front bands, and sleeve gussets are not felted.
- Coat is assembled after pieces are felted.

abbreviations

See page 141.

Delicata

SPECIAL ABBREVIATIONS

Hdc2tog: (Yo, insert hook in next st, yo and draw up a loop) twice, yo and draw through all 5 loops on hook.
Hdc3tog: (Yo, insert hook in next st, yo, draw up a loop) 3 times, yo and draw through all 7 loops on hook.
Shell: Work 3 dc in indicated st.
CGR (crossed group): Skip next Shell, work Shell in center st of following Shell, ch 3, working from left to right, Shell in center st of Shell just skipped.

SPECIAL STITCH

Woven Shell Stitch (Woven Shell st)
(Multiple of 6 sts)
Row 1: Ch 3 (counts as 1 dc), *skip next 3 sts, work Shell in next st, ch 3, working from left to right, work Shell in second of 3 sts just skipped, skip next st, dc in next st; rep from * to end, turn.
Row 2: Ch 3 (counts as 1 dc), work 3 dc in first st, sc in next ch-3 sp, *work CGR, sc in next ch-3 sp*; rep from * across, end work 4 dc in top of turning chain, turn.
Row 3: Ch 3 (counts as 1 dc), *work CGR, sc in next ch-3 sp; rep from * across, end dc in top of turning chain, turn.
Rows 4 and 5: Rep Rows 2 and 3.
Work Rows 1–5 for Woven Shell st.

COAT
BACK

Ch 74 (82, 90, 98, 106).
Row 1: Hdc in third ch from hook and in each ch across, turn (72 (80, 88, 96, 104) hdc).
Row 2: Ch 2, hdc in each st across, turn.
Rep Row 2 until 64 (64, 64, 68, 68) rows have been completed from beg. **Note:** piece should measure approx. 28 (28, 28, 30, 30)" (71.1 (71.1, 71.1, 76.2, 76.2)cm).

ARMHOLE SHAPING

Row 1: Sl st across first 12 sts, ch 2, hdc across to last 12 sts, turn leaving rem sts unworked (48 (56, 64, 72, 80) hdc). Work even for 22 (22, 26, 26, 26) rows more. **Note:** armhole should measure approx. 10 (10, 12, 12, 12)" (25.4 (25.4, 30.5, 30.5, 30.5)cm). Fasten off.

LEFT FRONT

Ch 26 (30, 34, 38, 42)
Row 1: Hdc in third ch from hook and in each ch across, turn (24 (28, 32, 36, 40) hdc).
Row 2: Ch 2, hdc in each st across. Turn. Rep Row 2 until 64 (64, 64, 68, 68) rows have been completed from beg; piece should measure approx. 28 (28, 28, 30, 30)" (71.1 (71.1, 71.1, 76.2, 76.2) cm).

ARMHOLE SHAPING

Row 1: Sl st across first 12 sts, ch 2, hdc across, turn (12 (16, 20, 24, 28) hdc). Work even for 22 (22, 26, 26, 26) rows more. **Note:** armhole should measure approx. 10 (10, 12, 12, 12)" (25.5 (25.4, 30.5, 30.5, 30.5) cm). Fasten off.

RIGHT FRONT

Work as for Left Front.

SLEEVES (Make 2.)

Note: work from the shoulder to the cuff.
Ch 66 (66, 78, 78, 78).
Row 1: Hdc in third ch from hook and in each ch across, turn (64 (64, 76, 76, 76) hdc).
Row 2: Ch 2, hdc in each st across, turn.
Rep Row 2 until 10 rows have been completed from beg. **Note:** piece should measure approx. 4½" (11.4cm) from beg.

SLEEVE SHAPING

Row 1: Ch 2, hdc2tog, hdc across to last 2 sts, end hdc2tog, turn (62 (62, 74, 74, 74) hdc).
Row 2: Ch 2, hdc in each st across, turn. Rep rows 1 and 2 until 40 (40, 48, 48, 48) sts rem.
Note: work even until 40 rows have been completed from beg. **Note:** piece should measure approx. 18" (45.7cm). Fasten off.

FINISHING

Weave in all loose ends.
(continued on page 38)

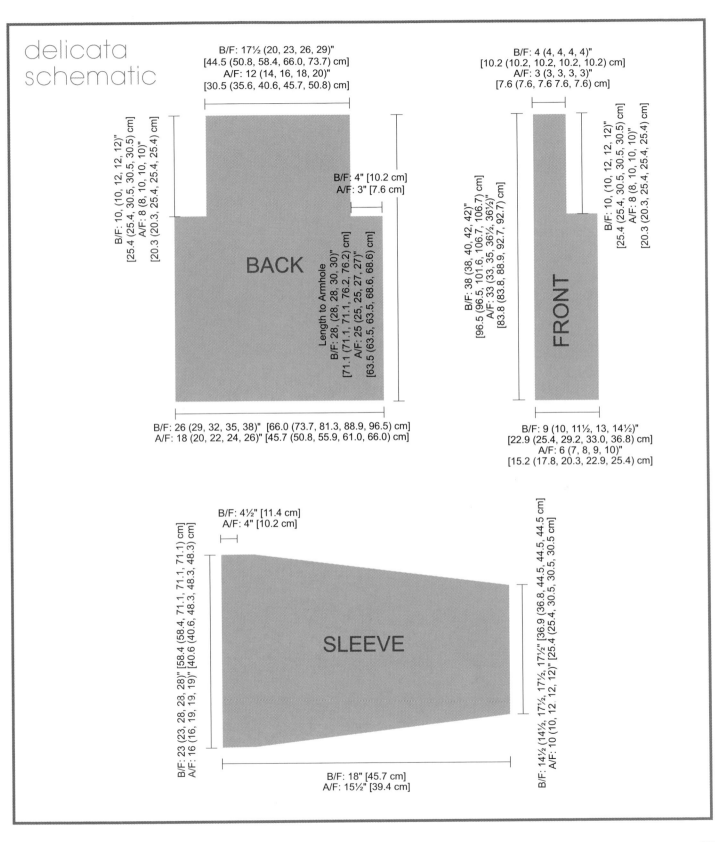

delicata schematic

BACK

B/F: 17½ (20, 23, 26, 29)"
[44.5 (50.8, 58.4, 66.0, 73.7) cm]
A/F: 12 (14, 16, 18, 20)"
[30.5 (35.6, 40.6, 45.7, 50.8) cm]

B/F: 10, (10, 12, 12, 12)"
[25.4 (25.4, 30.5, 30.5, 30.5) cm]
A/F: 8 (8, 10, 10, 10)"
[20.3 (20.3, 25.4, 25.4, 25.4) cm]

B/F: 4" [10.2 cm]
A/F: 3" [7.6 cm]

Length to Armhole
B/F: 28, (28, 28, 30, 30)"
[71.1 (71.1, 71.1, 76.2, 76.2) cm]
A/F: 25 (25, 25, 27, 27)"
[63.5 (63.5, 63.5, 68.6, 68.6) cm]

B/F: 26 (29, 32, 35, 38)" [66.0 (73.7, 81.3, 88.9, 96.5) cm]
A/F: 18 (20, 22, 24, 26)" [45.7 (50.8, 55.9, 61.0, 66.0) cm]

FRONT

B/F: 4 (4, 4, 4, 4)"
[10.2 (10.2, 10.2, 10.2, 10.2) cm]
A/F: 3 (3, 3, 3, 3)"
[7.6 (7.6, 7.6 7.6, 7.6) cm]

B/F: 10, (10, 12, 12, 12)"
[25.4 (25.4, 30.5, 30.5, 30.5) cm]
A/F: 8 (8, 10, 10, 10)"
[20.3 (20.3, 25.4, 25.4, 25.4) cm]

B/F: 38 (38, 40, 42, 42)"
[96.5 (96.5, 101.6, 106.7, 106.7) cm]
A/F: 33 (33, 35, 36½, 36½)"
[83.8 (83.8, 88.9, 92.7, 92.7) cm]

B/F: 9 (10, 11½, 13, 14½)"
[22.9 (25.4, 29.2, 33.0, 36.8) cm]
A/F: 6 (7, 8, 9, 10)"
[15.2 (17.8, 20.3, 22.9, 25.4) cm]

SLEEVE

B/F: 4½" [11.4 cm]
A/F: 4" [10.2 cm]

B/F: 23 (23, 28, 28, 28)" [58.4 (58.4, 71.1, 71.1, 71.1) cm]
A/F: 16 (16, 19, 19, 19)" [40.6 (40.6, 48.3, 48.3, 48.3) cm]

B/F: 14½ (14½, 17½, 17½, 17½)" [36.9 (36.8, 44.5, 44.5, 44.5 cm]
A/F: 10 (10, 12, 12, 12)" [25.4 (25.4, 30.5, 30.5, 30.5) cm]

B/F: 18" [45.7 cm]
A/F: 15½" [39.4 cm]

Delicata

(continued from page 37)

FELTING

See "Felting Basics" on pages 160 to 169. Check and measure the coat frequently during the felting process. Felt and block it to the after-felting (A/F) measurements listed in the schematic, and lay it flat to dry.

SLEEVE GUSSET (Not Felted)

Pick up first Sleeve. With RS facing, join yarn with sl st in left side edge of first row (at sleeve cap).

Row 1 (RS): Ch 2, work 2 hdc in side edge of same row as joining, *skip next row, work 2 hdc in side edge of next row; rep from * to end. Fasten off.

With RS facing, join yarn with sl st at cuff to work opposite side of Sleeve.
Row 1 (RS): Ch 2, work 2 hdc in side edge of same row as joining, *skip next row, work 2 hdc in side edge of next row; rep from *to end. Turn.
Rows 2–4: Ch 3, dc in each st across, turn. Fasten off.

ASSEMBLING
Sew shoulder seams. Sew side seams, leaving lower 3" (7.6cm) unstitched for side slits. Sew sleeve seams. Set Sleeves into armholes.

COLLAR AND FRONT BANDS (Not Felted)
With RS facing, join yarn with sl st in side edge of first row of Right Front edge.
Row 1 (RS): Ch 2, work 2 hdc in side edge of same row as joining, *skip next row, work 2 hdc in side edge of next row; rep from * to end taking care to have a multiple of 6 sts, turn.
Row 2: Ch 2, working in front loops only, hdc in each st to end, turn. Work Rows 1–5 of Woven Shell st.
Next row (RS): Ch 2, hdc in first 3 sts, *hdc3tog over next (dc, sc, dc), hdc in next 2 sts, work (hdc, ch 1, hdc) in next ch-3 sp, hdc in next 2 dc; rep from *, end hdc3tog over next (dc, sc, dc), hdc in last 2 sts, hdc in top of turning chain, turn. Fasten off.

With WS of Left Front facing, join yarn with sl st in side edge of Row 1.
Last row (WS): Ch 2, hdc evenly across side edge to first st of last row worked, work 2 hdc in first st, hdc in each st to first ch-1 sp, work (hdc, ch 1, hdc) in ch-1 sp, *hdc in next 2 sts, hdc2tog over next 2 sts, hdc in next 2 sts, work (hdc, ch 1, hdc) in next ch-1 sp; rep from*, end hdc to last st, work 2 hdc in last st, turn to side edge, hdc evenly spaced across side edge. Fasten off.

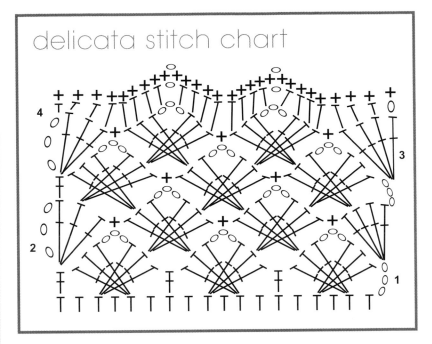

delicata stitch chart

"Delicata" is a coat of contrasts ~ the lace edging adds romantic style, while the smooth crocheted fabric adds contemporary flair. For a unique look, make the coat and the lace edging in contrasting colors.

Allotrope

THE ELEMENT CARBON IS CALLED AN ALLOTROPE BECAUSE IT CAN TAKE TWO FORMS—GRAPHITE, WHICH IS SOFT, OR DIAMOND, WHICH IS THE HARDEST NATURALLY OCCURRING MATERIAL KNOWN. WHILE FELTING IS CERTAINLY EASIER THAN TURNING CARBON INTO DIAMONDS, YOU CAN OBSERVE A SIMILAR MAGICAL TRANSFORMATION WHEN YOU FELT FABRIC. HERE, "ALLOTROPE," A FELTED AND CROPPED VEST, HAS A U-SHAPED NECK AND A FITTED WAIST THAT LOOKS GREAT WHEN LAYERED OVER A CAMI, BLOUSE, OR T-SHIRT.

Before Felting

After Felting

skill level

Intermediate

finished size*

(*completed vest after felting, blocking, assembling, and finishing)
- **X-Small:** 32" (81.3cm) bust and 23" (58.4cm) long
- **Small:** 35" (88.9cm) bust and 23" (58.4cm) long
- **Medium:** 38" (96.5cm) bust and 23" (58.4cm) long
- **Large:** 44" (111.8cm) bust and 25" (63.5cm) long
- **X-Large:** 47" (119.4cm) bust and 25" (63.5cm) long

before-felting (B/F) and after-felting (A/F) measurements

See schematic.

materials

- Brown Sheep Company Nature Spun Sport: 100% wool (184 yds. (168.2m) / 1¾ oz. (50g)), color #99 charcoal, 3 (3, 4, 4, 5) skeins

notions

- Tapestry needle

hook

- H/8 (5.00mm), or size needed to obtain gauge
- E/4 (3.50mm), or size needed to obtain gauge

gauge

- 13 hdc and 12 rows = 4" (10.2cm) before felting
- 13 hdc = 3" (7.6cm) and 12 rows = 3⅝" (9.0cm) after felting

notes

- Back and front are felted; front side gussets are not.
- Turning chain does not count as stitch.

abbreviations

See page 141.

SPECIAL ABBREVIATIONS

Hdc2tog: (Yo, insert hook in next st, yo and draw up loop) twice, yo and draw through all 5 loops on hook.

VEST

BACK

With larger hook, ch 67 (74, 80, 93, 100).
Row 1: Hdc in third ch from hook and in each ch across, turn (65 (72, 78, 91, 98) hdc).
Row 2: Ch 2, hdc in each st across, turn.
Rep Row 2 for pat st and work even until 40 (40, 40, 44, 44) rows have been completed from beg. **Note:** piece should measure approx. 13½ (13½, 13½, 14½, 14½)" (34.3 (34.3, 34.3, 36.8, 36.8)cm) from beg.

ARMHOLE SHAPING

Row 1: Sl st across first 9 (10, 10, 12, 13) sts, hdc across to last 9 (10, 10, 12, 13) sts, turn, leaving rem sts unworked (47 (52, 58, 67, 72) hdc).
Row 2: Ch 2, hdc2tog, hdc across to last 2 sts, end hdc2tog, turn (45 (50, 56, 65, 70) hdc).
Row 3: Ch 2, hdc in each st across, turn.
Rep Rows 2 and 3 a total of 4 (5, 6, 8, 9) times (39 (42, 46, 51, 54) hdc). Work even until armhole measures 7¾ (7¾, 7¾, 8¾, 8¾)" (19.7 (19.7, 19.7, 22.2, 22.2)cm).

RIGHT NECK SHAPING

Row 1 (RS): Hdc in first 5 (6, 8, 9, 10) sts, hdc2tog, turn leaving rem sts unworked (6 (7, 9, 10, 11) hdc).
Row 2: Ch 2, hdc across, turn.
Row 3: Ch 2, hdc in first 4 (5, 7, 8, 9) sts, hdc2tog, turn (5 (6, 8, 9, 10) hdc). Work even until armhole measures 12½ (12½, 12½, 13½, 13½)" (31.8 (31.8, 31.8, 34.3, 34.3)cm).
Fasten off.

LEFT NECK SHAPING

With RS facing, skip center 25 (26, 26, 29, 30) sts, join yarn with sl st in next st.
Row 1 (RS): Ch 2, hdc2tog working first hdc in same st as joining, hdc in last 5 (6, 8, 9, 10) sts, turn (6 (7, 9, 10, 11) hdc).
Row 2: Ch 2, hdc across, turn.
Row 3: Ch 2, hdc2tog, hdc across, turn (5 (6, 8, 9, 10) hdc). Work even until armhole measures 12½ (12½, 12½, 13½, 13½)" (31.8 (31.8, 31.8, 34.3, 34.3)cm).
Fasten off.

FRONT

Work as for Back to Armhole Shaping.

ARMHOLE AND U-NECK SHAPING

Row 1: Sl st across first 9 (10, 10, 12, 13) sts, ch 2, hdc across next 11 (13, 16, 19, 21) sts, hdc2tog, turn, leaving rem 43 (47, 50, 58, 62) sts unworked, (12 (14, 17, 20, 22) hdc).
Cont to shape Armhole same as for Back. AT THE SAME TIME, cont to dec 1 st at neck edge every other row 3 times more, (5 (6, 8, 9, 10) hdc).
Work even until U-neck measures 13½ (13½, 13½, 14½, 14½)" (34.3 (34.3, 34.3, 36.8, 36.8)cm).
Fasten off.

LEFT NECK SHAPING

With RS facing, skip center 21 (22, 22, 25, 26) sts, join yarn with sl st in next st.
Row 1 (RS): Ch 2, hdc2tog working first hdc of the dec in same st as joining, hdc in next 11 (13, 16, 19, 21) sts, turn. leaving rem 9 (10, 10, 12, 13) sts unworked (12 (14, 17, 20, 22) hdc).
Cont to shape Armhole same as for Back. AT THE SAME TIME, cont to dec 1 st at neck edge every other row 3 times more, (5 (6, 8, 9, 10) hdc).
Work even until armhole measures 12½ (12½, 12½, 13½, 13½)" (31.8 (31.8, 31.8, 34.3, 34.3)cm).
Fasten off.

FINISHING

Weave in all loose ends.

FELTING

See "Felting Basics" on pages 160 to 169. Check and measure your vest frequently during the felting process. Felt and block to the after-felting (A/F) measurements listed in the schematic. Lay the vest flat to dry.

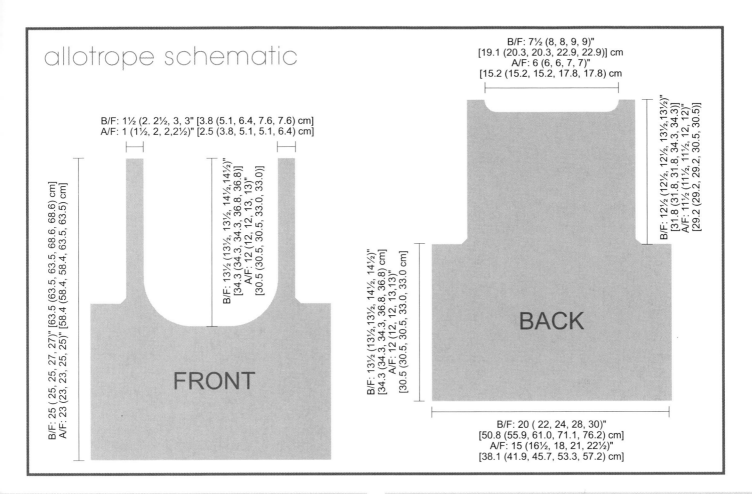

allotrope schematic

FRONT

B/F: 1½ (2, 2½, 3, 3" [3.8 (5.1, 6.4, 7.6, 7.6) cm]
A/F: 1 (1½, 2, 2,2½)" [2.5 (3.8, 5.1, 5.1, 6.4) cm]

B/F: 13½ (13½, 13½, 14½, 14½)"
[34.3 (34.3, 34.3, 36.8, 36.8)]
A/F: 12 (12, 12, 13, 13)"
[30.5 (30.5, 30.5, 33.0, 33.0)]

B/F: 25 (25, 25, 27, 27)" [63.5 (63.5, 63.5, 68.6, 68.6) cm]
A/F: 23 (23, 23, 25, 25)" [58.4 (58.4, 58.4, 63.5, 63.5) cm]

BACK

B/F: 7½ (8, 8, 9, 9)"
[19.1 (20.3, 20.3, 22.9, 22.9)] cm
A/F: 6 (6, 6, 7, 7)"
[15.2 (15.2, 15.2, 17.8, 17.8) cm

B/F: 12½ (12½, 12½, 13½,13½)"
[31.8 (31.8, 31.8, 34.3, 34.3)]
A/F: 11½ (11½, 11½, 12, 12)"
[29.2 (29.2, 29.2, 30.5, 30.5)]

B/F: 13½ (13½,13½, 14½, 14½)"
[34.3 (34.3, 34.3, 36.8, 36.8) cm]
A/F: 12 (12, 12, 13, 13)"
[30.5 (30.5, 30.5, 33.0, 33.0 cm]

B/F: 20 (22, 24, 28, 30)"
[50.8 (55.9, 61.0, 71.1, 76.2) cm]
A/F: 15 (16½, 18, 21, 22½)"
[38.1 (41.9, 45.7, 53.3, 57.2) cm]

FRONT SIDE GUSSETS (Not Felted)

With RS of Front facing, join yarn with sl st in right side edge of first row.

Row 1 (RS): Ch 1, sc evenly across side edge to Armhole Shaping, turn.

Row 2: Ch 2, hdc in each st across, turn.

Rows 3 and 5: Ch 2, working in back loops only, hdc in each st across, turn.

Rows 4 and 6: Ch 2, working in front loops only, hdc in each st across, turn.

Row 7: Rep Row 2. Fasten off, leaving 18" (45.7cm) end for sewing.

With RS of Front facing, join yarn with sl st in left side edge of last row before Armhole Shaping.

Beg with Row 1, cont to work as for opposite side edge.

Note: use the gusset to customize the fit, making it narrower or wider according to your preference.

BACK SIDE EDGING (Not Felted)

With RS of Back facing, join yarn with sl st in right side edge of first row.

Row 1 (RS): Ch 1, sc evenly across side edge to Armhole Shaping. Fasten off.

With RS of Back facing, join yarn with a sl st in left side edge of last row before Armhole Shaping.

Rep Row 1 as for opposite side edge.

ASSEMBLING

Sew the shoulder seams. Sew the side seams.

NECK EDGING (Not Felted)

With RS facing, join yarn with sl st in center back neck edge.

Rnd 1: Ch 1, sc evenly around neck edge, join rnd with sl st in first st. Fasten off.

ARMHOLE EDGING (Not Felted)

With RS facing, join yarn with sl st in center of underarm.

Rnd 1: Ch 1, sc evenly around armhole edge, join rnd with sl st in first st. Fasten off. Weave in rem loose ends.

Picot Fan

The appeal of "Picot Fan" is the pretty stitch used to create the feathery, fan-shape edging on the shrug. Added after the body of the shrug is crocheted, the lacy detail lends a romantic, vintage feel to the piece. A shrug is a bit of crochet mystery—a simple rectangle becomes a garment when it is folded and sewn at opposite edges to form sleeves. After felting, the shawl collar and cuffs of "Picot Fan" are crocheted in the round, adding texture and style.

skill level

Intermediate

finished size*

(*completed shrug after felting, blocking, assembling, and finishing)
- **Small/Medium:** fits 32"–36" (81.3cm–91.4cm) bust
- **Large/X-Large:** fits 38"–44" (96.5cm–111.8cm) bust

before-felting (B/F) and after-felting (A/F) measurements

See schematic.

materials

- Classic Elite Lush: 50% angora, 50% wool (124 yds. (113.4m) / 1¾ oz. (50g)), color #4420 aqua foam, 10 (12) skeins

notions

- Tapestry needle
- Safety pins

hooks

- H/8 (5.00mm), or size needed to obtain gauge
- G/6 (4.00mm), or size needed to obtain gauge

gauge

- 10 hdc and 9 rows = 4" (10.2cm) before felting
- 10 hdc and 9 rows = 3½" (8.9cm) after felting

notes

- Body of shrug is felted.
- Edgings are not felted.
- Shrug is assembled after felting.
- Turning chain does not count as stitch.

abbreviations

See page 141.

Before Felting

After Felting

Picot Fan

SPECIAL STITCHES

Half Double Crochet Cluster (hdc-cl): Yarn over, insert hook into next st, yo, pull up loop, yo, insert hook back into same st, yo, pull up loop, yo and pull through all 5 loops.

PICOT-FAN STITCH

(Multiple of 12 sts)

Rnd 1 (RS): Ch 1, sc in first st, *ch 5, skip next 3 sts, sc in next st; rep from *around, join rnd with sl st in first sc.

Rnd 2: Sl st to third ch of first ch-5 sp, ch 1, sc in same ch, *work 8 dc in next ch-5 sp, sc in next ch-5 sp, ch 5, sc in next ch-5 sp; rep from *around to last ch-5, sc in last ch-5 sp, ch 2, hdc in first sc to join (counts as ch-5 sp).

Rnd 3: Ch 1, sc in same ch-5 sp, *dc in next dc, (ch 3, sl st in 3rd ch from hook (picot made) dc in next dc) 7 times, sc in next ch-5-sp; rep from * around, join rnd with sl st in first sc to join.

Rnd 4: Ch 8 (counts as 1 dc and ch 5), skip first 2 picots, * sc in next picot, ch 5, skip next picot, sc in next picot, ch 5, skip next 2 picots, dc into next sc, ch 5 skip 2 picots; rep from * around, join rnd with a sl st in third ch of beg ch-8.

Rnds 5 and 6: Rep Rnds 2 and 3.

Work Rnds 1–6 for Picot Fan st.

SHRUG

BODY

With larger hook, ch 72 (92) loosely.

Row 1: Hdc-cl in third ch from hook and in each ch across, turn (70 (90) hdc-cl).

Row 2: Ch 2, hdc-cl in each st across (do not work in tch), turn. (70 (90,) sts).

Rep Row 2 until piece measures 32 (34)" (81.3 (86.4)cm) from beg. Fasten off.

FINISHING

Weave in all loose ends.

Mark the foundation edge using a scrap of cotton yarn.

FELTING

See "Felting Basics" on pages 160 to169. Check and measure your shrug frequently during the felting process. Felt and block to the after-felting (A/F) measurements listed in the schematic, and lay the shrug flat to dry.

ASSEMBLING

With the foundation edge at the bottom, locate and mark the center 8" (20.3cm) on the top and bottom edges using safety pins. **Note:** this is the armhole. With RS facing, fold the piece in half lengthwise. Sew the side seams, leaving the 8" armhole (20.3cm) opening on each side.

BODY EDGING (Not Felted)

With RS facing and smaller hook, join yarn with sl st in center of

flirty...

one long edge (this is now the center back neck edge).

Foundation Rnd: Ch 1, work 240 (276) sc evenly spaced around entire outer edge.

LACE PATTERN

Work Rnds 1–6 of Picot Fan st. Fasten off.

ARMHOLE EDGING (Not Felted)

With RS facing and smaller hook, join yarn with sl st in underarm seam.

Foundation Rnd: Ch 1, work 72 sc evenly spaced around entire armhole edge.

LACE PATTERN

Work Rnds 1–6 of Picot Fan st. Fasten off. Weave in remaining loose ends.

…and fun

picot-fan schematic

Sew side edges together

Armhole 8" [20.3 cm]

Folding Edge (Fold in half)

B/F: 32 (34)" [81.3 (86.4) cm]
A/F: 28 (30)" [71.0 (76.2) cm]

B/F: 28 (36)" [71.1 (91.1) cm]
A/F: 24½ (31½)" [62.2 (80.0) cm]

Sew side edges together

picot-fan stitch chart

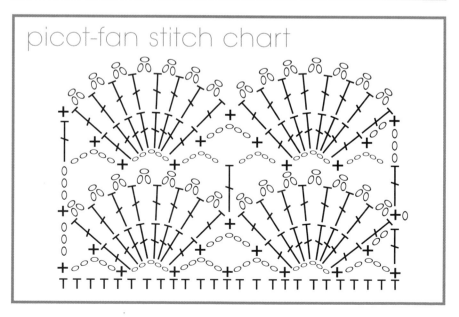

Siberian Jewel

THIS TOQUE-STYLE HAT WAS INSPIRED BY TRA-DITIONAL FUR CAPS WORN IN RUSSIA. WORKED IN A SOFT MOHAIR YARN, THE CROCHETED FAB-RIC HAS THE LOOK OF ACTUAL FUR. MOHAIR IS ONE OF THE LIGHTEST ANIMAL FIBERS, AND IT IS OFTEN USED TO ADD LOFT TO HEAVIER YARNS. THE AMETHYST COLOR OF THE YARN EVOKES THE COLD, HARSH CLIMATE WHERE THE AMETHYST GEMSTONE IS FOUND. IN THIS PROJ-ECT, THE CROCHETED SHAPE IS HARD-FELTED, CREATING A SOLID AND STURDY FABRIC THAT HELPS MAINTAIN THE STRUCTURE OF THE HAT.

Before Felting

After Felting

skill level

Elementary

finished size*

(*completed hat after felting and blocking)
- 22" (55.9cm) circumference and 6" (15.2cm) from crown to brim; fits an average woman's head

before-felting (B/F) measurements

- 30" (76.2cm) circumference and approx. 8" (20.3cm) from crown to brim

materials

- Be Sweet Mohair Bouclé: 100% baby mohair (120 yds. (109.7m) / 1¾ oz. (50g)), color pale amethyst, 4 skeins

notions

- Tapestry needle
- Bowl or container (for mold)

hook

- M/13 (9.00mm), or size needed to obtain gauge

gauge

- 9½ hdc and 6 rows = 4" (10.2cm) before felting with two strands held together
- 9½ hdc and 6 rows = 3" (7.6cm) after felting

notes

- Hat is worked in the round in one piece.
- Hat is worked with two strands of yarn held together throughout.
- Turning chain does not count as stitch.

abbreviations

See page 141.

Siberian Jewel

HAT

Holding two strands of yarn together, ch 5. Join ch with sl st to form ring.

CROWN

Rnd 1: Ch 2, work 12 hdc in ring, join rnd with sl st in first st (12 hdc).

Rnd 2: Ch 2, hdc in first st, work 2 hdc in next st, *hdc in next st, work 2 hdc in next st; rep from * around, join rnd with sl st in first st (18 hdc).

Rnd 3: Ch 2, hdc in each st around, join rnd with sl st in first st.

Rnd 4: Rep Rnd 2 (27 hdc).

Rnd 5: Rep Rnd 3.

Rnd 6: Ch 2, hdc in first st, work 2 hdc in next st, * hdc in next st, work 2 hdc in next st; rep from * around to last st, work 2 hdc in last st, join rnd with sl st in first st (41 hdc).

Rnd 7: Rep Rnd 3.

Rnd 8: Rep Rnd 6 (62 hdc).

Rnd 9: Ch 2, hdc in first 7 sts, work 2 hdc in next st, * hdc in next 7 sts, work 2 hdc in next st; rep from * around to last 6 sts, hdc in next 5 sts, work 2 hdc in last st, join rnd with sl st in first st (70 hdc).

Rnd 10: Ch 2, working in back loops only, hdc in each st around, join rnd with sl st in first st.

BRIM

Rnds 11–21: Ch 2, hdc in each st around, join rnd with sl st in first st.

Fasten off.

FINISHING

Weave in all loose ends.

FELTING

See "Felting Basics" on pages 160 to 169. The hat is hard-felted. Felt the hat, checking it often for fit. **Note:** the hat should fit snugly on the crown of your head. Block the hat over a bowl or container, shaping it as shown or as desired. Let the hat dry thoroughly.

OPTIONAL

If the hat is very "hairy," trim off the excess fibers using sharp scissors.

trimming the fiber

The height of the pile on felted fabric can be made shorter if you like the look of a lower pile on your hat. First, use a hair brush with fine wire bristles, such as a new dog brush, and a scooping motion to lift up the yarn fibers. Then use sharp scissors to trim the fibers to an even length. Work one section of the felted fabric at a time.

Fashionable and versa~ tile, "Siberian Jewel" is a chic accessory that will flatter you with style. For a daytime look, wear it with a cropped jacket or fun coat. For an understated evening look, make the hat in a rich black yarn, adding a pin for extra sparkle.

Andean
Scarf & Mittens

This pretty scarf, one part of a scarf-and-mitten set, draws inspiration from the airy fleece of the alpaca whose coat ranges in color from creamy white to dark-chocolate brown. A perfect accent for wardrobe pieces in any style, the set can be made in more intense colors. Consider making the pair in alpaca that is dyed a rich purple and wearing it with a black-and-white herringbone jacket. Or match the yarn color of the scarf and mittens to an outfit for subtle style.

ANDEAN SCARF

skill level

Elementary

finished size*

(*completed scarf after felting and blocking)
• 53" (1.3m) long and 8" (20.3cm) wide

before-felting (B/F) measurements

• 56" (1.4m) long and 10" (25.4cm) wide

materials

• Blue Sky Alpacas Sportweight: 100% baby alpaca (110 yds. (100.5m) / 1¾ oz. (50g)), color #500 natural white, 4 skeins

notions

• 1½" (38mm) round button, color as desired
• Embroidery floss or yarn (to match button)
• Tapestry needle and straight pins

hook

• K/10½ (6.50mm), or size needed to obtain gauge

gauge

• 14 hdc and 10 rows = 4" (10.2cm) before felting
• 14 hdc = 3" (7.6cm) and 10 rows = 3½" (8.9cm) after felting

notes

• Scarf is crocheted, then felted.
• Turning chain does not count as stitch.

abbreviations

See page 141.

Before Felting

After Felting

Andean Scarf

SPECIAL ABBREVIATIONS

Hdc2tog: (Yo, insert hook in next st, yo and draw up loop) twice, yo and draw through all 5 loops on hook.

Hdc3tog: (Yo, insert hook in next st, yo and draw up loop) 3 times, yo and draw through all 7 loops on hook.

SCARF

Ch 2.

Row 1: Work 3 hdc in 2nd ch from hook, turn.

Row 2: Ch 2, work 2 hdc in first st, hdc in next st, work 2 hdc in last st, turn (5 hdc).

Row 3: Ch 2, work 2 hdc in first st, hdc in each st to last st, work 2 hdc in last st, turn (7 hdc).

Rep Row 3 until you have 35 hdc. Work even in hdc until piece measures 49" (1.2m) from beg.

END SHAPING

Row 1: Ch 2, hdc2tog, hdc in each st to last 2 sts, hdc2tog, turn (33 hdc).

Rep Row 1 until 3 sts rem.

Last Row: Ch 2, hdc3tog.

Do not fasten off; turn to side edge.

PICOT EDGING

Rnd 1 (RS): Ch 1, *work (sc, ch 8, sc) in side edge of next row, skip next row; rep from * around entire edge, join rnd with a sl st in first sc.

Fasten off.

FINISHING

Weave in all loose ends.

FELTING

See "Felting Basics" on pages 160 to 169. Scarf is hard-felted. Check and measure the scarf frequently during the felting process. If you prefer a soft-felted effect, remove the scarf from the tub of the washing machine when the stitches can still be distinguished. Block the scarf to the finished-size measurements listed in the materials list, and lay it flat to dry.

SEWING BUTTONHOLE

Wrap the scarf around your neck, adjusting it so that it is comfortable. Use a straight pin to indicate the desired placement of the buttonhole. (Look at the photograph for guidance.) Cut the buttonhole slightly smaller than the diameter of the button; then carefully enlarge the slit if necessary. Use embroidery floss or yarn to whipstitch around the edge of the buttonhole opening to prevent fraying. Using the buttonhole as a guide, sew the button to opposite end of the scarf.

CROCHET A BUTTON

Use a slip knot to anchor a length of yarn to a plastic ring that is slightly smaller than the buttonhole. With your crochet hook, work single crochet stitches around the ring to conceal it completely; do not cut the yarn. Thread the end of the yarn through a tapestry needle, and sew diagonal stitches across the ring to fill the center space. Exit the center of the "web" of stitches; then sew the button to the scarf. Fasten off.

A scarf may be the last thing you put on, but it is one of the more important elements that can make a personal style statement ～ whether you wrap the scarf around your neck, allow it to cascade in long streamers, or tie it in an oversized knot. A scarf can be the one accessory that establishes the tone of your personal style.

Andean Mittens

skill level

Elementary

finished size*

(*completed mittens after felting and blocking)
- 8½" (21.6cm) hand circumference
  and 8½" (21.6 cm) long; fits an average woman's hand

before-felting (B/F) measurements

- 11½" (29.2cm) hand circumference and 11" (27.9cm) long

materials

- Blue Sky Alpacas Sportweight: 100% baby alpaca
  (110 yds. (100.5m) / 1¾ oz. (50g)), color #500 natural
  white, 4 skeins

notions

- Tapestry needle

hook

- K/10½ (6.50mm), or size needed to obtain gauge

gauge

- 11 hdc and 11 rows = 4" (10.2cm) before felting
- 11 hdc and 11 rows = 3" (7.6cm) after felting

notes

- Mittens are crocheted, then felted.

abbreviations

See page 141.

special abbreviation

Hdc2tog: (Yo, insert hook in next st, yo, and draw up a loop)
twice, yo, and draw through all 5 loops on hook.

MITTENS

(Make 2.)
Ch 32. Join ch with sl st forming ring, turn.
Rnd 1: Ch 2, hdc in same ch as joining, hdc in next 31 ch around, join rnd with sl st in first st (32 hdc).
Rnd 2: Ch 2, hdc in each st around, join rnd with sl st in first st. Rep Rnd 2 until piece measures 3" (7.6cm) from beg, turn.

THUMB OPENING: LEFT HAND

Rows 1–4: Ch 2, hdc in next 28 sts, turn leaving rem 4 sts unworked.
Joining Rnd: Ch 2, hdc in next 28 sts, ch 4, join rnd with sl st in first st.

THUMB OPENING: RIGHT HAND

Row 1: Sl st across first 4 sts, ch 2, hdc in next 28 sts, turn, leaving sl st unworked.
Rows 2–4: Ch 2, hdc in next 28 sts, turn.
Joining Rnd: Ch 2, hdc in next 28 sts, ch 4, join rnd with sl st in first st.

CONTINUE FOR BOTH HANDS

Rnd 1: Ch 2, hdc in next 28 sts, hdc in next 4 ch, join rnd with sl st in first st (32 hdc).
Rnds 2–11: Ch 2, hdc in each st around, join rnd with sl st in first st.

TOP SHAPING

Rnd 1: Ch 2, hdc2tog, hdc in next 12 sts, (hdc2tog) twice, hdc in next 12 sts, hdc2tog, join rnd with sl st in first st (28 hdc).
Rnd 2: Ch 2, hdc2tog, hdc in next 10 sts, (hdc2tog) twice, hdc in next 10 sts, hdc2tog, join rnd with sl st in first st (24 hdc).
Rnd 3: Ch 2, hdc2tog, hdc in next 8 sts, (hdc2tog) twice, hdc in next 8 sts, hdc2tog, join rnd with a sl st in first st (20 hdc).
Rnd 4: Ch 2, hdc2tog, hdc in next 6 sts, (hdc2tog) twice, hdc in next 6 sts, hdc2tog, join rnd with sl st in first st (16 hdc).
Rnd 5: Ch 2, hdc2tog, hdc in next 4 sts, (hdc2tog) twice, hdc in next 4 sts, hdc2tog, join rnd with sl st in first st (12 hdc).
Rnd 6: Ch 2, hdc2tog, hdc in next 2 sts, (hdc2tog) twice, hdc in next 2 sts, hdc2tog, join rnd with sl st in first st (8 hdc). Fasten off, leaving 6" (15.2cm) end. Thread end into tapestry needle, and weave through rem sts. Pull tight to gather.
Fasten off.

Mittens are practical accessories that can add flare to any outerwear, and when you add such bouncy details as pom-poms, they are more fun to wear. Use matching yarn to make two small pom-poms about one inch in diameter for each mitten. Sew them to the outside edge of the cuff.

super soft...

...and toasty warm

THUMB

With RS facing, join yarn with sl st in first st of thumb opening.

Rnd 1: Ch 2, hdc in same st as joining, hdc in next 3 sts, work 3 hdc along side edge of opening, working through bottom loops of ch, hdc in next 4 bottom loops, work 3 hdc along side edge of opening, join rnd with sl st in first st (14 hdc).

Rnds 2–7: Ch 2, hdc in each st around, join rnd with sl st in first st.

THUMB SHAPING

Rnd 1: Ch 2, (hdc2tog) 7 times, join rnd with sl st in firt st (7 hdc).

Rnd 2: Ch 2, hdc in first st, (hdc2tog) three times, join rnd with sl st in first st (4 hdc).

Fasten off leaving a 6" (15.2cm) end. Thread end into tapestry needle, and weave through rem sts. Pull tight to gather.

Fasten off.

FINISHING (Picot Edging)

With RS facing, and working in bottom loops of foundation ch, join yarn with sl st in any bottom loop.

Rnd 1 (RS): Ch 1, work (sc, ch 8, sc) in same bottom loop as joining, skip next bottom loop, *work (sc, ch 8, sc) in next bottom loop, skip next bottom loop; rep from * around, join rnd with sl st in first sc. Fasten off. Weave in all ends.

FELTING

See "Felting Basics" on pages 160–169. Check and measure your mittens frequently during the felting process. Felt and block the mittens to after-felting (A/F) measurements listed in the materials list, and lay them flat to dry.

Note: the mittens will shed a lot. If desired, allow them to go through the machine's high-spin cycle for one minute to remove excess water. Stand up the mittens to dry them.

Vivids

THE MOOD OF THE PROJECTS IN THIS CHAPTER IS BOLD AND ASSERTIVE. BRIGHT COLORS INSPIRE FEELINGS OF PRIDE, CONFIDENCE, JOY, AND EXCITEMENT. RED IS PASSIONATE; YELLOW IS INTELLECTUAL, CAUSING THE VIEWER TO FOCUS INWARD; ORANGE IS CREATIVE AND COMBINES THE HUES OF RED AND YELLOW IN DIFFERING PROPORTIONS; BLUE IS THE COLOR OF HEALING AND IS ALSO ASSOCIATED WITH TRUTH, LOYALTY, AND HONOR; GREEN EVOKES BIRTH AND NEW BEGINNINGS. BLACK IS RICH AND MYSTERIOUS AND CAN BE A BACKDROP THAT SETS OFF ANY OTHER COLOR USED WITH IT.

VIVID COLORS PLAY OUT IN THE DRAMATIC "AMARANTH," A JACKET THAT HAS A SLIM SILHOUETTE AND AN OVERSIZED "FUR" COLLAR TO ADD TEXTURAL INTEREST, AND IN "TARTAN," A PLAID BAG THAT EVOKES THE SCOTTISH HIGHLANDS WITH ITS STRONG LINES AND GEOMETRIC PATTERNING. FOR WHIMSY, BLACK AND WHITE INFORM "PEONY," A TOTE-STYLE BAG WITH SCULPTED EDGING THAT INTRODUCES BOLD CONTRASTS—ITS APPLIQUÉD-FELT FLOWER IN WHITE POPS CHEERILY OFF A SOLID BLACK BACKGROUND. PINK DEFINES THE SHAPE OF "CORAL REEF," A SHRUG THAT HAS A VINTAGE FEEL. BRIGHT BERRY HIGHLIGHTS THE FLIRTY KNEE-LENGTH SKIRT "WINE AND ROSES"—ITS SLIM SILHOUETTE ACCENTED BY A CORSAGE OF CROCHETED ROSES THAT COULD EASILY MAKE ITS WAY ONTO ANY ENSEMBLE.

Coral Reef

A shrug is a wonderful project to create if you want to experiment with stitches, texture, and color. Made from a simple rectangle, "Coral Reef" is a portable project that can be brought on vacation and to visits with friends. Because there is no shaping and there are no unusual elements of construction, you'll be free to focus on the stitch—a beautiful pinwheel. Crocheted in a luscious wool-and-angora yarn, the shrug is as soft and satisfying to crochet as it is to wear.

skill level

Intermediate

finished size*

(*completed shrug after felting, blocking, assembling, and finishing)
- **Small/Medium:** 32"-38" (81.3cm-96.5cm) bust; 35" (88.9cm) circumference of body
- **Large/X-Large:** 40"-44" (101.6cm-111.8cm) bust; 41" (104.1cm) circumference of body

before-felting (B/F) and after-felting (A/F) measurements

See schematic.

materials

- Classic Elite Lush: 50% angora, 50% wool (124 yds. (113.4m) / 1¾ oz. (50g)), color #4480 Coral, 12 (14) skeins

notions

- Tapestry needle; safety pins

hooks

- H/8 (5.00mm), or size to obtain gauge
- G/6 (4.25mm) for edging

gauge

- 27 sts and 5 rows of body st pattern = 7" (17.8cm) x 4" (10.2cm) before felting
- 27 sts and 5 rows of body st pattern = 6" (15.2cm) x 3¾" (9.5cm) after felting

notes

- Body and sleeves are crocheted, then felted; shell edging is added after assembly and is not felted

abbreviations

See page 141.

Before Felting

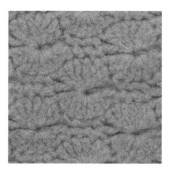

After Felting

Coral Reef

SPECIAL STITCHES
CL (cluster): Work (yo, insert hook, yo, draw yarn through 2 loops) over the number of stitches indicated, yo, draw through all loops on hook.

SHELL EDGING PATTERN
Note: this edging should be worked evenly along the edge of the shrug into the space created by the tch-sp. Work 5 hdc in tch-sp, * ch 1, work 5 hdc in next tch-sp, rep from * to end of round, sl st to beg to join.

SHRUG
BODY STITCH PATTERN (Body st pat)
(Multiple of 10 sts + 6; add 1 for base chain.)
Row 1: Sc into second ch from hook, sc into next ch, * skip 3 ch, 7 dc into next ch, skip 3 ch, sc into each of next 3 ch, rep from * to last 4 ch, skip 3 ch, 4 dc into last ch, turn.
Row 2: Ch 1, sc into first st, sc into next st, *ch 3, CL over next 7 sts, ch 3, sc into each of next 3 sts, rep from * to last 4 sts, ch 3, CL over last 4 sts, skip tch, turn.
Row 3: Ch 3 (counts as 1 dc), 3 dc into first st, * skip 3 ch, sc into each of next 3 sc, skip 3 ch, 7 dc into top of next CL, rep from * to end, finishing with (skip 3 ch, sc into each of last 2 sc, skip tch), turn.
Row 4: Ch 3 (counts as 1 dc), skip first st, CL over next 3 sts, * ch 3, sc into each of next 3 sts, ch 3, CL over next 7 sts, rep from * finishing with ch 3, sc into next st, sc into top of tch, turn.
Row 5: Ch 1, sc into each of first 2 sc, * skip 3 ch, 7 dc into top of next CL, skip 3 ch, sc into each of next 3 sc, rep from * ending skip 3 ch, 4 dc into top of tch, turn.
Rep Rows 2–5 for pat.

BODY
With larger hook, ch 107 (137).
Follow Body st pat, and work until piece measures 37 (43)" (93.9 (109.4)cm) from beg. Fasten off.

SLEEVES (Make 2.)
Ch 67 sts. Follow Body st pat, and work until piece measures 9 (11)" (27.9 (25.4) cm) from foundation. Fasten off. Weave in all ends.

FELTING
See "Felting Basics" on pages 160 to 169. Check and measure your pieces frequently during the felting process. Felt and block the pieces to the after-felting (A/F) measurements listed in the schematic, and lay them flat to dry.

ASSEMBLING
Fold the Body in half lengthwise, and use safety pins to mark the center point on each side edge. Unfold the Body, and lay it flat. Fold the Sleeves in half, matching the foundation edge to the final row; use safety pins to mark the center point on the side edge of each Sleeve. Center the marked points on the Body to the marked points on the Sleeves. Sew the shoulder seams. Fold the shrug in half. Sew the Sleeves and side seams in one line.

EDGING (Not Felted)
With smaller hook, work Shell Edging Pattern evenly around the body opening and the sleeve edging.

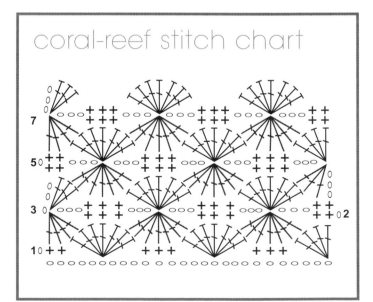

coral-reef stitch chart

coral-reef schematic

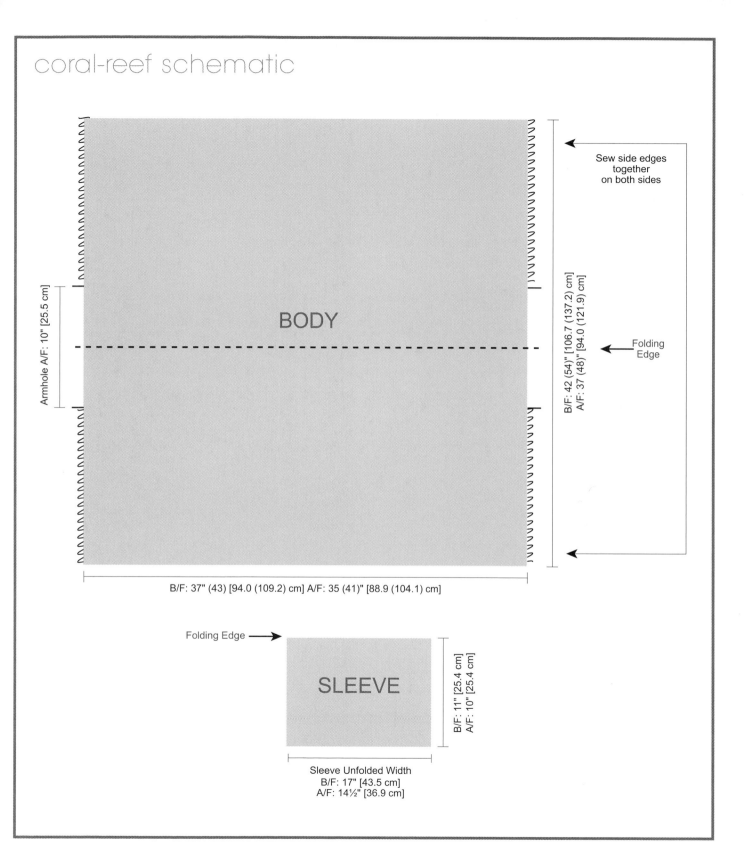

Sew side edges
together
on both sides

Folding Edge

Armhole A/F: 10" [25.5 cm]

BODY

B/F: 42 (54)" [106.7 (137.2) cm]
A/F: 37 (48)" [94.0 (121.9) cm]

B/F: 37" (43) [94.0 (109.2) cm] A/F: 35 (41)" [88.9 (104.1) cm]

Folding Edge →

SLEEVE

B/F: 11" [25.4 cm]
A/F: 10" [25.4 cm]

Sleeve Unfolded Width
B/F: 17" [43.5 cm]
A/F: 14½" [36.9 cm]

Peony

THE PEONY IS A SYMBOL OF BASHFULNESS, AND IT IS SAID TO BE A "FICKLE" FLOWER THAT WHEN MOVED WILL NOT OPEN AGAIN FOR YEARS. THE FLOWER ON THIS TOTE IS ANYTHING BUT BASHFUL. ITS OVERSIZED PETALS AND LEAVES ARE CLUSTERED TOGETHER TO CREATE A BOLD FLORAL ACCENT ON THE BAG. BECAUSE THE BLOOM IS CUT FROM SEPARATE FELTED PIECES, "PEONY" IS A GREAT BEGINNER PROJECT.

Before Felting

After Felting

skill level

Elementary

finished size*

(*completed bag after assembling, felting, and blocking)
- 34" (86.4cm) around and 15" (38.1cm) high (from base to opening)

before-felting (B/F) measurements

- 45" (114.3cm) around (or 22½" (58.1cm) wide) and 17" (43.2cm) high (from base to opening)

materials

- Patons Classic Wool: 100% wool, (223 yds. (204.9cm) / 3½ oz. (100g)), MC: # 0026 black, 4 skeins; CC1: # 0202 Aran; and CC2: 00240 Leaf Green, one skein of each

notions

- Stitch marker
- 2 plastic handles as shown or as desired
- ½ yd. (0. 4m) fabric (for lining)
- 1 sheet of plastic canvas (to reinforce bag bottom and upper edge)
- Pins: safety; straight
- Tapestry needle
- Permanent fabric glue

hooks

- H/8 (5.00mm), or size needed to obtain gauge
- J/10 (6.00mm) for stems on flowers

gauge

- 14 hdc over 11 rows = 4" (10.2cm) before felting
- 14 hdc = 3" (7.6cm) and 11 rows = 3½" (8.9cm) after felting

notes

- Bag is crocheted in two pieces (sides and bottom).
- Bag sides and bottom are sewn together before felting.
- Flower and leaf appliqués are created from fabric that is crocheted, felted, and then cut into required shapes using template on page 67.
- Felted appliqués are sewn onto bag after it is felted.
- Handles and lining are attached during finishing.
- Turning chain does not count as stitch.

abbreviations

See page 141.

special abbreviations

Hdc2tog Group: Yo, insert hook in next ch, yo and pull up loop, yo, skip 3 ch, insert hook in next ch, yo and pull up loop, yo and pull through 5 loops on hook.
V-Stitch (V-st): (Hdc, ch1, hdc) in same stitch.

Peony

PATTERN NOTE

Bag: worked in rounds and in chevron pattern, which consists of 10 rounded points at the top edge.

BAG

With MC and smaller hook, ch 160 loosely, sl st in first ch, being careful not to twist chain.

Rnd 1 (Setup Round): Ch 1, * hdc into each of next 5 ch, hdc2tog group, hdc into each of next 5 ch, V-st in next ch, rep from * 9 more times, end with sl st in first st (10 V-sts).

Rnd 2: Ch 1, hdc in first st, hdc into each of next 4 sts, * hdc2tog, hdc into each of next 5 hdc, V-st into ch-1 sp, hdc into each of next 5 hdc, rep from * around, end with V-st in ch-1 sp, sl st in first st.

Rep Rnd 2 until piece measures 17" (43.2cm).

Final Rnd: Ch 1, rev sc in each st around, place marker in final round to mark top of bag.

BOTTOM

With MC and smaller hook, ch 17.

Row 1: Hdc in second ch from hook and in each ch across, turn (16 hdc).

Row 2: Ch 1, hdc in each st across, turn.

Repeat Row 2 until piece measures 18" (45.7cm). Weave in all ends.

FLOWER AND LEAVES

(Make 2 pieces, one using CC1 and one using CC2.)
With smaller hook, ch 51.
Row 1: Hdc in second ch from hook and in each ch across, turn (50 hdc).
Row 2: Ch 1, hdc in each st across, turn.
Rep Row 2 until piece measures 15" (38.1cm).
Weave in all ends.

STEMS

(Make 3.)
With double strand of CC2 and larger crochet hook, ch 35. Fasten off.

ASSEMBLING

Attach the bottom to the bag as follows:
using double strand of MC and a tapestry needle, sew the bottom edge of the bag's sides to the edge of the bag's bottom. Center one chevron point over each side edge of the bag.

FINISHING
FELTING

See "Felting Basics" on pages 160 to 169. The bag is hard-felted. Check and measure the bag fequently during the felting process. Felt and block the bag to the measurements indicated in the materials list. Use books covered in plastic to hold the shape of the bag while it is drying. Because the bag is hard-felted, it may take more than one cycle to produce the desired felted effect.

Felt the flower, leaves, and stem pieces in their own wash cycle so that the colors do not bleed. Put each of the sections of the appliqué in a mesh bag to keep them from getting lost.

HANDLES AND LINING

Center the handles on the inside edge of the front and the back of the bag. Sew them on.
Cut the plastic canvas to fit the bottom and the sides of the bag, and glue them in place inside the bag.
Cut the lining to size, and sew it into the bag.

FLOWER AND LEAVES

Enlarge the templates (top right) according to the marked sizes, and use them to cut out the petals and the leaves from the felted fabric. Sew the petals in a cluster to make the flower; then add the leaves. Sew the crocheted chain onto the leaves as shown.

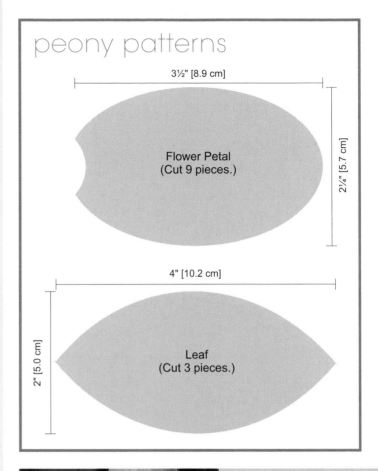

peony patterns

3½" [8.9 cm]

2¼" [5.7 cm]

Flower Petal
(Cut 9 pieces.)

4" [10.2 cm]

2" [5.0 cm]

Leaf
(Cut 3 pieces.)

RED IS THE COLOR OF STARDOM—
ON THE STAGE, ONLY THE LEAD
ACTRESS WEARS RED. YOU CAN
TAKE THE LEAD IN "WINE &
ROSES," A DRAMATIC PENCIL SKIRT
CROCHETED IN THE ROUND,
USING SIMPLE STITCHES AND
EASY SHAPING. THE SKIRT HAS A
VERY SUBTLE FLOUNCE AT THE
EDGE OF THE HEM AND SHAPING
AT THE HIPS AND WAIST. THE
"RED-ROSE CORSAGE PIN" ADDS
A FLIRTY-AND-FUN LOOK.

Before Felting

After Felting

SKIRT

skill level

Intermediate

finished size*

(*completed skirt after felting, assembling, and finishing)

- **X-Small:** 28" (71.1cm) waist and 35" (88.9cm) hip
- **Small:** 30" (76.2cm) waist and 37" (93.9cm) hip
- **Medium:** 33" (83.8cm) waist and 40" (101.6cm) hip
- **Large:** 36" (91.4cm) waist and 43" (109.2cm) hip
- **X-Large:** 40" (101.6cm) waist and 46" (116.8cm) hip
- **2X-Large:** 44" (111.8cm) waist and 48" (121.9cm) hip

- **Length 1:** 27½" (69.9cm)
- **Length 2:** 31" (78.7cm)
- **Length 3:** 34" (86.4cm)

before-felting (B/F) and after-felting (A/F) measurements

See schematic.

materials

- Brown Sheep Nature Spun Sport: 100% wool (184 yds. (168.2m) / 1¾ oz. (50g)), color #N48S Scarlet, 8 (9, 9, 10, 10, 11) skeins

notions

- 1–2 yds. (0.9m–1.8m) elastic, 1" (2.5cm) wide (for waistband)
- Tapestry needle
- 2 removable stitch markers

hooks

- G/6 (4.25mm), or size needed to obtain gauge
- F/5 (3.75mm), or size needed to obtain gauge

gauge

- 20 hdc and 12 rows = 4" (10.2cm) before felting
- 20 hdc and 12 rows = 3½" (8.9cm) after felting

notes

- Skirt is worked in the round from top down in one piece.
- Rounds are joined with sl st.
- Turning chain does not count as stitch.
- Waistband is lightly felted; then it is sewn to skirt.
- Red-Rose corsage is crocheted separately; then it is sewn to skirt.

abbreviations

See page 141.

special abbreviations

Hdc-bl: Half double crochet in back loop only.
Hdc2tog: (Yo, insert hook into next st and pull up loop) twice, yo and pull through 5 loops on hook.

Wine & Roses

SKIRT

With larger hook, ch 160 (180, 190, 210, 230, 250), sl st in first ch to join, being careful not to twist chain.

Rnd 1: Ch 1, * hdc in next 80 (90, 95, 105, 115, 125) sts, pm in last st worked, rep from * once more, sl st in first st to join.

Rnd 2: Ch 1, 2 hdc in first hdc, * hdc in each hdc to st before marker, 2 hdc in marked st, move marker to hdc just made, 2 hdc in next hdc, rep from * around, ending 2 hdc in marked st, move marker to hdc just made, sl st in first hdc to join (164 (184, 194, 214, 234, 254) hdc).

Rep Rnd 2 until you have total of 200 (220, 242, 250, 270, 282) hdc.

Work even in hdc until piece measures 9" (22.8cm) from beg, continue to move marker up with each rnd.

BEGIN SKIRT DECREASES

Continue working in hdc, but begin to dec (hdc2tog) every third row before and after each marker until 180 (180, 190, 190, 190, 190) hdc remain. Work even until skirt is the desired length following before-felting (B/F) measurements for length 1, 2, or 3 as listed on the schematic. **Note:** the skirt will shrink 5"–7" (12.7cm–17.8cm) in length when it is felted.

WAISTBAND

With smaller hook, ch 21.

Row 1: Hdc in second ch from hook, and in each ch across, turn (20 hdc).

Row 2: Ch 1, hdc-bl in each st across, turn.

Rep Row 2 until piece measures 26 (28, 31, 34, 38, 42)" (66.0 (71.1, 78.7, 86.4, 96.5, 106.7) cm) or desired length.

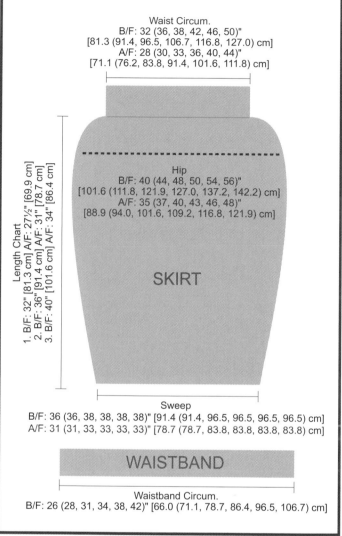

wine & roses schematic

Waist Circum.
B/F: 32 (36, 38, 42, 46, 50)"
[81.3 (91.4, 96.5, 106.7, 116.8, 127.0) cm]
A/F: 28 (30, 33, 36, 40, 44)"
[71.1 (76.2, 83.8, 91.4, 101.6, 111.8) cm]

Hip
B/F: 40 (44, 48, 50, 54, 56)"
[101.6 (111.8, 121.9, 127.0, 137.2, 142.2) cm]
A/F: 35 (37, 40, 43, 46, 48)"
[88.9 (94.0, 101.6, 109.2, 116.8, 121.9) cm]

SKIRT

Length Chart
1. B/F: 32" [81.3 cm] A/F: 27½" [69.9 cm]
2. B/F: 36" [91.4 cm] A/F: 31" [78.7 cm]
3. B/F: 40" [101.6 cm] A/F: 34" [86.4 cm]

Sweep
B/F: 36 (36, 38, 38, 38, 38)" [91.4 (91.4, 96.5, 96.5, 96.5, 96.5) cm]
A/F: 31 (31, 33, 33, 33, 33)" [78.7 (78.7, 83.8, 83.8, 83.8, 83.8) cm]

WAISTBAND

Waistband Circum.
B/F: 26 (28, 31, 34, 38, 42)" [66.0 (71.1, 78.7, 86.4, 96.5, 106.7) cm]

FINISHING

Weave in all ends. Sew short ends of waistband together.

FELTING

See "Felting Basics" on pages 160 to 169. Check and measure your skirt frequently during the felting process. Felt and block the skirt to the measurements listed in the schematic, and lay the skirt flat to dry. Lightly hand-felt the waistband—just enough to "fuzz" the stitches but not enough to change the size of the waistband.

CORSAGE PIN

finished size*

(*completed single blooms in different sizes)
Large: approx. 3" (7.6cm) in diameter
Small: approx. 2½" (6.4cm) in diameter

materials

- DMC Pearl Cotton Embroidery Thread: size 3, 100% cotton; 16 yds. (14.6m), color #498 and #814, 2 skeins each; color #815, #3350, and #326, 1 skein each.

notions

- Pin backings, 2 or more as desired; small tapestry needle; scrap of felt, large enough for multiple roses

hook

- Steel crochet hook #6 (1.80mm), or size needed to obtain gauge

gauge

- Rounds 1–7 will make a rose 2" (6.4cm) in diameter

notes

- Work roses as follows:
  - 3 small roses with 4 rounds of petals: first in #815; second in #3350; and third in #326
  - 2 large roses with 6 rounds of petals: first in #498; and second in #814

abbreviations

See page 141.

ASSEMBLING

Sew the waistband to the skirt, using yarn and a tapestry needle. Attach the elastic, using the crochet casing stitch as follows: with smaller hook, sl st below where you'd like elastic to lie, ch up and over elastic, and sl st chain to skirt just above elastic. Continue to chain back and forth over elastic in a zigzag pattern. **Note:** this method creates a secure casing for the elastic without adding bulk. If your elastic twists, tack it to the inside of the waistband with matching thread.

CORSAGE PIN

For large and small rose, ch 6, sl st in first st to make ring.
Rnd 1: (Sc, hdc, dc, tr, dc, hdc) 5 times into ring (5 petals).
Rnd 2: Working behind petals, sl st around middle of tr post in first petal, (ch 3, sc around middle of tr post in next petal) 5 times (5 ch-3 lps).
Rnd 3: Work (sc, hdc, dc, tr, dc, hdc, sc) in each loop around.
Rnd 4: Working behind petals, sl st around middle of tr post in first petal, (ch 4, sc around middle of tr post in next petal) 5 times (5 ch-4 lps).
Rnd 5: Work (sc, hdc, 2 dc, tr, 2 dc, hdc, sc) in each loop around.
Rnd 6: Working behind petals, sl st around middle of tr post in first petal, (ch 5, sc around middle of tr post in next petal) 5 times (5 ch-5 lps).
Rnd 7: Work (sc, hdc, 3 dc, tr, 3 dc, hdc, sc) in each loop around.
For small rose, end here by fastening off.
Note: for large rose, continue following the directions below.

LARGE ROSE

Rnd 8: Working behind petals, sl st around middle of tr post in first petal, (ch 6, sc around middle of tr post in next petal) 5 times (5 ch-6 lps).
Rnd 9: Work (sc, hdc, 2 dc, 3 tr, 2 dc, hdc, sc) in each loop around.
Rnd 10: Rep Rnd 8.
Rnd 11: Work (sc, hdc, 2 dc, 5 tr, 2 dc, hdc, sc) in each loop around, sl st in first sc to join.
Fasten off.

FINISHING

Weave in ends.

ASSEMBLING

To make the pin as shown, arrange the flowers on a scrap of felt using the photograph of the corsage as a guide.

If you want the flowers to be removable, pin them to the felt. If you want the flowers to be permanent, tack down each of the roses using a tapestry needle and matching thread. Sew the pin backings onto the backside of the felt scrap.

Amaranth

THE BRIGHT-PINK COLOR OF THE AMARANTH FLOWER WAS PRIZED BY THE HOPI INDIANS WHO USED THE PIGMENT FROM THE PETALS AS A DYE. HERE, THE PRETTY COLOR AMARANTH NAMES A JACKET THAT IS MADE FROM WARM WOOL USING A TUNISIAN STITCH (TO KEEP THE FELT PLIABLE). THE JACKET IS FITTED FOR GREAT STYLE AND TOPPED WITH A DRAMATIC LOOPED COLLAR.

Before Felting

After Felting

skill level

Advanced

finished size*

(*completed jacket after felting, blocking, assembling, and finishing)
- **X-Small:** 30" (76.2cm) bust and 20" (50.8cm) long
- **Small:** 34" (86.4cm) bust and 20" (50.8cm) long
- **Medium:** 38" (96.5cm) bust and 20" (50.8cm) long
- **Large:** 42" (106.7cm) bust and 22" (55.8cm) long
- **X-Large:** 46" (116.8cm) bust and 22" (55.8cm) long

before-felting (B/F) and after-felting (A/F) measurements

See schematic.

materials

- **MC:** Cascade Yarns ECO +; 100% Peruvian Highland wool (478 yds. (437.1m) / 8¾ oz. (250g)), color #6913 Fuchsia, 3 (3, 3, 4, 4) skeins

- **CC:** Gedifra Gigante; 100% new wool (33 yds. (30.2m) / 1¾ oz. (50g)), color #2358, 3 skeins for all sizes

notions

- 13"–14" (33.0cm–35.6cm) separating zipper

- 1 pair size 11 (8.00mm) knitting needle (for collar)

hooks

- K/10½ (6.5mm) Tunisian/Afghan hook 14" (35.6cm) long, or size needed to obtain gauge
- J/10 (6.0mm), or size needed to obtain gauge

gauge

- 12 Tss and 10 rows = 4" (10.2cm) before felting
- 12 Tss and 10 rows = 3½" (8.9cm) after felting

notes

- Body and sleeves are worked in Tunisian simple stitch pattern.
- Pieces are crocheted and felted, then sewn together and finished.
- Collar is not felted and is worked with CC after jacket is felted.

abbreviations

See page 141.

special abbreviations

Tss: Tunisian simple stitch
Tss2tog: (decrease) to decrease one stitch on Forward row, insert hook through two stitches to be decreased, pull up 1 loop.
For detailed instructions in Tunisian Crochet, see the leg-warmer pattern, "Jambières," on page 122.

Amaranth

14" (35.6cm). Starting with next Forward row, Tss2tog. Tss across 20 (23, 26, 29, 32) sts, leaving 5 sts unworked. Tss2tog at beg of every Forward row until 18 sts remain. Work even in Tss until armhole measures 9 (9, 9, 12, 12)" (22.9 (22.9, 22.9, 30.5, 30.5)cm). Fasten off.

SLEEVES
(Make 2.)
Ch 60 (60, 72, 72, 72). Work even in Tss for 1" (2.5cm).

SLEEVE SHAPING
Row 1: Tss2tog, work in Tss to last 2 stitches, Tss2tog.
Rows 2–3: Work even in Tss.
Rep Rows 1–3 until 38 stitches remain, continue to work even in Tss until Sleeve measures 24 (24, 26, 26, 26)" (61.0 (61.0, 66.0, 66.0)cm). Fasten off.

FELTING
See "Felting Basics" on pages 160 to169. Check and measure your pieces frequently during the felting process. Felt and block the pieces to the after-felting (A/F) measurements listed in the schematic, and lay them flat to dry.

JACKET
BACK
With MC and Tunisian hook, ch 54 (60, 66, 72, 78). Work even in Tss until piece measures 14" (35.6cm), turn.

ARMHOLE SHAPING
Sl st 5 sts, Tss across 44 (50, 56, 62, 68) sts, leaving 5 sts unworked. Work even in Tss until armhole measures 9 (9, 9, 12, 12)" (22.9 (22.9, 22.9, 30.5, 30.5)cm). Fasten off.

LEFT FRONT
With MC and Tunisian hook, ch 27 (30, 33, 36, 39). Work even in Tss until piece measures 14" (35.6cm).

ARMHOLE SHAPING
Sl st 5 sts Tss across 20 (23, 26, 29, 32), Tss2tog. Tss2tog at end of every Forward row until 18 sts remain.
Work even in Tss until armhole measures 9 (9, 9, 12, 12)" (22.9 (22.9, 22.9, 30.5, 30.5)cm). Fasten off.

RIGHT FRONT
Work as for Left Front until piece measures

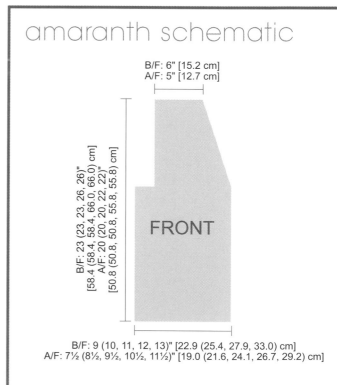

amaranth schematic

B/F: 6" [15.2 cm]
A/F: 5" [12.7 cm]

B/F: 23 (23, 23, 26, 26)" [58.4 (58.4, 58.4, 66.0, 66.0) cm]
A/F: 20 (20, 20, 22, 22)" [50.8 (50.8, 50.8, 55.8, 55.8) cm]

FRONT

B/F: 9 (10, 11, 12, 13)" [22.9 (25.4, 27.9, 33.0) cm]
A/F: 7½ (8½, 9½, 10½, 11½)" [19.0 (21.6, 24.1, 26.7, 29.2) cm]

ASSEMBLING

Sew the shoulder seams. Set in the sleeves. Sew the sleeve and side seams. Attach the zipper.

FINISHING
COLLAR (Not Felted)

Worked in rounds using CC.

With J/10 (6.00mm) hook, work loose chain approx. length of neckline from one side of front, around back, and down to other side of front at top of zipper. Work looped collar as follows:

*Hold knitting needle in right hand behind crochet hook, yo 3 times on needle. Insert crochet hook in next ch and work sc, remove knitting needle to create loop of yarn.

Rep from * across length of chain.

Then flip chain over, and rep process across back edge of chain. Flip chain over again, and work a second round in same way, working into sc sts instead of chain.

Continue working rounds of loop stitch until collar is 4" (10.1cm) wide or as desired.

Sew collar into neck opening.

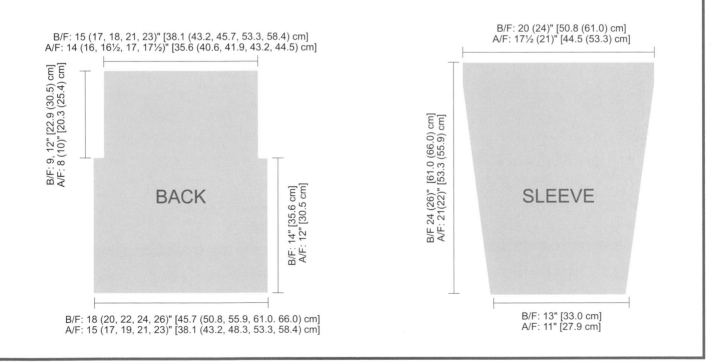

B/F: 15 (17, 18, 21, 23)" [38.1 (43.2, 45.7, 53.3, 58.4) cm]
A/F: 14 (16, 16½, 17, 17½)" [35.6 (40.6, 41.9, 43.2, 44.5) cm]

B/F: 9, 12" [22.9 (30.5) cm]
A/F: 8 (10)" [20.3 (25.4) cm]

BACK

B/F: 14" [35.6 cm]
A/F: 12" [30.5 cm]

B/F: 18 (20, 22, 24, 26)" [45.7 (50.8, 55.9, 61.0. 66.0) cm]
A/F: 15 (17, 19, 21, 23)" [38.1 (43.2, 48.3, 53.3, 58.4) cm]

B/F: 20 (24)" [50.8 (61.0) cm]
A/F: 17½ (21)" [44.5 (53.3) cm]

B/F: 24 (26)" [61.0 (66.0) cm]
A/F: 21(22)" [53.3 (55.9) cm]

SLEEVE

B/F: 13" [33.0 cm]
A/F: 11" [27.9 cm]

Snowberry

If you're lucky, a walk in a wintry wood might not be devoid of bright color if you come upon the pink-and-red blooms of the snowberry bush before its white berries have burst forth, sending them to the ground. Here, our "Snowberry" mittens evoke the same colorful blooms— a pretty mix that shifts from pale pink and raspberry to cream and chocolate brown. As the variegated yarn is worked, it forms a fabric that has pleasing patches of contrasting color.

Before Felting

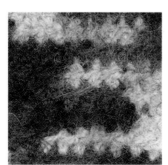

After Felting

skill level

Elementary

finished size*

(*completed mittens after felting and blocking)
- 9" (22.9cm) hand circumference and 9½" (24.1cm) long; one size fits most women.

before-felting (B/F) measurements

- 10" (25.4cm) hand circumference and 10½" (26.7cm) long

materials

- Patons Classic Wool: 100% pure new wool, (223 yds. (203.9m), 3½ oz. (100g)), color #77414 Rosewood, 1 skein

notions

- Tapestry needle

hook

- H/8 (5.00mm) crochet hook, or size needed to obtain gauge

gauge

- 12 hdc and 10 rows = 4" (10.2cm) before felting
- 12 hdc and 10 rows = 3¾" (9.5cm) after felting

notes

- Mittens are worked in rounds from cuff to fingers in one piece.

abbreviations

See page 141.

Snowberry

SPECIAL ABBREVIATIONS
Hdc2tog: (yo, insert hook into next st and draw up a loop) twice, yo and pull through 5 loops on hook.

MITTENS
(Make 2.)
Ch 30, sl st to first ch to form a ring, being careful not to twist chain.
Rnd 1: Ch 1, sc in first ch, ch 1, hdc in each of next 29 ch, sl st in first sc to join (30 sts).

Rnds 2–10: Ch 2, sc in first ch, ch 1, hdc in each of next 29 sts, sl st in first sc to join.

THUMB HOLE (Worked in rows)
Row 1: Sl st across first 2 sts, hdc in each of next 26 hdc, turn, leaving rem sts unworked (26 hdc).
Row 2: Ch 1, hdc in each st across, ch 4, sl st in first st to join, turn (30 sts).

TOP OF PALM (Continue in rounds)
Rnd 1: Ch 1, work hdc in each st and ch around, sl st in first hdc to join (30 hdc).
Rnds 2–5: Work in even rnds of hdc.

TOP OF MITTEN SHAPING
Rnd 1: Hdc across next 13 sts, hdc2tog, hdc in each of next 13 hdc, hdc2tog, sl st in first st to join (28 hdc).
Rnd 2: Hdc in each st to dec st from row below, hdc2tog, hdc around to last 2 sts, hdc2tog, sl st in first st to join (26 hdc).
Rep Rnd 2 until 14 sts remain.
Final decrease rnd: (Hdc2tog) 7 times, sl st to join

STYLE TIP
Mittens do not have to be plain-Jane. They can be dressed up by adding a band of lace around the cuffs. Use a yarn in a matching color, or select a yarn in a wildly contrasting color for a funky look. For inspiration, refer to the picot-fan stitch pattern featured in the "Picot Fan" shrug on page 44.

playful and

(7 hdc). Fasten off.

Note: leave at least a 6" (15.2cm) tail. Thread the tail into the yarn needle, and weave through rem sts, draw up tightly, and fasten securely.

THUMB

Rnd 1: Join yarn at thumb opening, work 12 hdc evenly around thumb opening, sl st in first st to join. Work even in hdc for 5 more rnds.

Final thumb rnd: (Hdc2tog) 6 times, sl st in first st to join (6 hdc). Fasten off. Thread the tail into the yarn needle, and weave it through the rem sts; draw up tightly; and fasten securely.

Weave in all remaining ends.

FELTING

See "Felting Basics" on page 160 to 169. Felt the mittens to the finished-size measurements listed in the materials list or until the mittens reach a desired size. Block the mittens, and allow them to dry standing up.

sporty

Friendship Mittens~ Make a mitten template from paper by tracing around your friend's hand. Enlarge the template according to the percentage of shrinkage that occurs with your yarn. Crochet the mittens using the enlarged template; then felt the mittens to the size of the original paper template.

Tartan

TARTAN PATTERNS HAVE A HISTORY THAT IS CENTURIES OLD, BUT IT WAS ONLY IN THE EIGHTEENTH CENTURY THAT UNIQUE PATTERNS WERE FORMALIZED AND ASSIGNED TO SPECIFIC CLANS IN SCOTLAND. NOW YOU CAN WEAR YOUR VERY OWN TARTAN PATTERN BY MAKING THIS BEAUTIFUL BAG. ITS CROCHETED FABRIC MIMICS THE LOOK OF A GENUINE TARTAN PLAID, BUT HERE THE EFFECT IS ACHIEVED BY WEAVING DOUBLE STRANDS OF YARN THROUGH THE FABRIC. FELTING PERMANENTLY "LOCKS" THE STRANDS IN THE FABRIC.

skill level

Intermediate

finished sizes*

(*completed crocheted rectangle after felting and blocking)
• 24" (61.0cm) long and 16" (40.6cm) wide
(*completed bag after assembling)
• 12" (30.5cm) high and 16" (40.6cm) wide

before-felting (B/F) measurements

• 28" (71.1cm) long and 16" (40.6cm) wide

materials

• Patons Classic Merino Wool: 100% pure new wool, (223 yds. (203.9m) / 3½ oz. (100g)), 4 skeins, one in each of the following colors:
MC: #226 Black; CC1: #202 Aran; CC2: #240 Leaf; and CC3: #77014 Forest (Multi)

notions

• 3 men's belts, all size large
• ½ yd. (45.7cm) fabric (for lining)
• Permanent fabric glue
• Needles: tapestry; upholstery; upholstery thread

hooks

• G/6 (4.25mm), or size needed to obtain gauge

gauge

• 17 sts (9 hdc, 8 ch total) and 10 rows = 4" (10.2cm) before felting
• 17 sts (9 hdc, 8 ch total) and 10 rows = 3½" (8.9cm) after felting

notes

• Weaving is done on unfelted fabric.

abbreviations

See page 141.

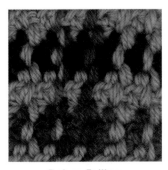

Before Felting

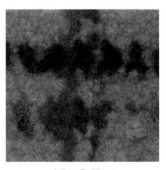

After Felting

Tartan

BAG
Note: bag is assembled from one crocheted rectangle.
With CC2, ch 80.
Row 1: Hdc into the fourth ch from hook. * ch 1, skip next ch, hdc in next ch: rep from * to end, turn.
Row 2: Ch 3 (counts as hdc and ch-1), skip first st, * hdc in next hdc, ch 1, rep from * across, ending with hdc in last hdc, turn (38ch-1 sps).

Following color sequences below, repeat row 2.
6 rows of CC2
**6 rows of CC3
2 rows of CC2
1 row of CC1
2 rows of CC2
2 rows of MC
2 rows of CC2
Rep from ** once more.

*** 6 rows of CC3.
2 rows of CC2
2 rows of MC
2 rows of CC2
1 row of CC1
2 rows of CC2
Rep *** once more.
End with 6 more rows of CC2.

BAG OPENING
Row 1: Hdc in each st and ch-1 sp across, turn.
Rows 2–7: Work even in hdc.
Turn bag, and join yarn to opposite edge of bag at foundation row. Ch 1, hdc in each ch across, turn.
Rep Rows 2–7 for bag opening. Fasten off.

WEAVING
On the rectangle of crocheted fabric, weave contrasting yarns alternately under and over the crocheted stitches using a threaded tapestry needle.

With the wrong side of the crocheted fabric facing you, begin weaving in the mesh rows from side to side using a tapestry needle threaded with a 40" (10.2m) double-strand of yarn. **Note:** you will weave two strands of yarn into each crocheted row.

Begin the first double-strand going over, then under the posts of the stitches; then weave the second double-strand in the opposite direction, going under, then over the posts of the stitches. Continue from side to side for the entire width of the fabric.

VERTICAL WEAVING
Begin the first double-strand, weaving vertically between the hdc stitches in ch-sps, going over, then under the rows of stitches; then weave the second double-strand in the opposite direction, going under the rows, then over them. Alternate the colors as follows:
**1 row MC
2 rows CC2
1 row CC1
5 rows CC3
1 row CC1
2 rows CC2.
rep from ** across, ending with 1 row of Black.

FINISHING
Weave in ends.

FELTING
See "Felting Basics" on pages 160 to 169. Check and measure the fabric frequently. Felt and block the fabric rectangle to the finished-size measurements listed in the materials list.

LINING
Cut a lining that is the same size as the blocked fabric. Fold over 1/4" (6mm) edges on each side of the lining, and iron them flat. Sew the lining to the wrong side of the bag fabric along the edges.

ASSEMBLING
Note: bag is assembled after felting.
Fold bag fabric in half with right sides together. Sew the side seams using a threaded tapestry needle. Turn the bag right side out.

ATTACHING THE SHOULDER STRAP
Cut off the buckle of one belt. Cut a second belt at the opposite end, leaving the buckle attached. Using the photo, opposite, as a guide, center one belt over each side seam of the bag so that the cut end of each belt is even with the base of the bag. Glue the belts to the bag along the seams, and buckle the opposite ends to complete the shoulder strap.

ATTACHING THE CLOSURE
Measure the circumference of the bag, beginning at the opening and wrapping all the way around; add 8" (20.3cm) to the measurement; cut the remaining belt to that length. Reposition and glue the decorative tip of the belt to the new cut end. Then center and wrap the belt around the bag as shown. Glue the belt to the bag, leaving the non-buckle end that extends over the bag opening unglued. Buckle the belt to secure the bag. **Optional:** glue any excess length of belt across the bag as shown.

Sew the edges of the belt to the bag using a sharp upholstery needle and upholstery thread.

The "Tartan" bag will become a staple in your wardrobe of accessories. Its smart pattern and functional shape will make it the "go~any~where" bag. If you prefer, choose yarn colors that go with the basics in your wardrobe.

Sand and Sea

THE BRIGHT-BLUE WOOL OF THIS SKIRT IS IN WONDERFUL CONTRAST TO THE SAND-COLORED WAISTBAND. TOGETHER THE COLORS EVOKE IMAGES OF BEAUTIFUL BEACHES AND CLEAR, COOL WATERS. "SAND AND SEA" WORKS UP QUICKLY IN THE ROUND, AFTER WHICH THE SKIRT IS FELTED TO A PERFECT FIT. THE WAISTBAND IS ADDED AFTER FELTING FOR A COMFORTABLE, STYLISH ACCENT.

Before Felting

After Felting

skill level

Intermediate

finished size*

(*completed skirt after felting, assembling, and finishing)
- **X-Small:** 28" (71.1cm) waist and 35" (88.9cm) hip
- **Small:** 30" (76.2cm) waist and 37" (93.9cm) hip
- **Medium:** 33" (83.8cm) waist and 40" (101.5cm) hip
- **Large:** 36" (91.5cm) waist and 43" (109.2cm) hip
- **X-Large:** 40" (101.5cm) waist and 46" (116.8cm) hip
- **2X-Large:** 44" (111.8cm) waist and 48" (121.9cm) hip

- Length 1: 25½" (64.8cm)
- Length 2: 24" (61.0cm)
- Length 3: 20" (50.8cm)

before-felting (B/F) and after-felting (A/F) measurements

See schematic.

materials

- **MC:** Cascade Yarns 220 Wool Quatro; 100% Peruvian wool (220 yds. (201.2m) / 3½ oz. (100g)), color #9434, 3 (3, 3, 4, 4, 4) skeins for length 2 and 3; 4 (4, 4, 5, 5, 5) skeins for length 1
- **CC:** Cascade Yarns Fixation; 98.3% cotton, 1.7% elastic (186 yds. (170.0m) / 1¾ oz. (50g)), color #7360, 2 skeins.

notions

- 7" (17.8cm) non-separating zipper
- Tapestry needle
- Sewing thread (to match yarns)
- Hand-sewing needle
- Removable stitch markers
- Optional: belt buckle

hooks

- I /9 (5.50mm), or size needed to obtain gauge
- J/10 (6.00mm) 10" (25.4cm) Tunisian/Afghan hook, or size needed to obtain gauge

gauge

- 12 hdc and 12 rows = 4" (10.2cm) square before felting
- 12 hdc and 12 rows = 3½" (8.9cm) after felting

notes

- Skirt is worked from waist down.
- Skirt is felted before elastic waistband is attached.
- Waistband is not felted.
- Elastic waistband is sewn onto foundation edge.

abbreviations

See page 141.

Sand and Sea

SPECIAL ABBREVIATIONS

Hdc-bl: Half double crochet in the back loop only
Hdc2tog: (Yo, insert hook into next st and pull up a loop) twice, yo and pull through 5 loops on hook.
Tss: Tunisian simple stitch
Tps: Tunisian purl stitch

SPECIAL STITCH

Belt Stitch Pattern (Belt st pat)
Row 1: Work (Tss in next st, Tps in next st) across. Work standard return row.
Rep Row 1 for pattern.
Note: for more detailed instructions for the Tunisian sts (Tss and Tps), see the leg warmers, "Jambières," on page 122.

SKIRT

Using standard crochet hook and MC, ch 96 (108, 114, 126 138, 150), slip st in first ch to join, being careful not to twist chain.
Rnd 1: Ch 1, *work 48 (54, 57, 63 69, 75) hdc, place marker, rep from * once more. Sl st in first st to join.
Rnd 2: Ch 1, 2hdc in first st, * hdc in each st to 2 sts before marker, 2 hdc in st before marker, 2 hdc in in st

before marker, hdc in marked st, 2 hdc in st after marker, rep from * once more, ending hdc in marked stitch, sl st in first st to join.
Rep Rnd 2 until you have 120 (132, 142, 150 162, 170) hdc. Work even until skirt is the desired length following before-felting (B/F) measurements for Length 1, 2, or 3 as listed on the schematic.

BELT

With MC, Ch 11.
Row 1: Hdc in second ch from hook work and in each ch across, turn. (10 hdc)
Row 2: Ch1, hdc in each st across, turn.
Rep Row 2 until belt is desired length.

BELT LOOPS

With MC, Ch 11.
Row 1: Hdc in second ch from hook and in each ch across.
Fasten off.
Sew the belt loops evenly onto the waistband.
Optional: attach a buckle to the belt, or tie the belt to close it.

FINISHING

Weave in all ends.

FELTING

See "Felting Basics" on pages 160 to 169. Check and measure your skirt frequently during the felting process. Felt and block the skirt to the after felting (A/F) measurements listed in the schematic, and lay the skirt flat to dry. Lightly felt the belt and belt loops just enough to "fuzz" the stitches.

ASSEMBLING

WAISTBAND (Not Felted)

With two strands of CC held together and the Tunisian/Afghan hook, make a chain that is long enough for your waist when it is stretched.
Continuing with two strands of yarn together, work in Belt st pat for 4" (10.2cm). Break off the yarn. Using yarn, sew the waistband into the skirt, placing the edges at the center of the back.

ZIPPER

Cut a 2½-in. (6.4cm) slit on the skirt directly below the opening for the zipper. Pin the zipper to the skirt and the waistband opening. If necessary, enlarge the zipper opening; then sew the zipper into place.

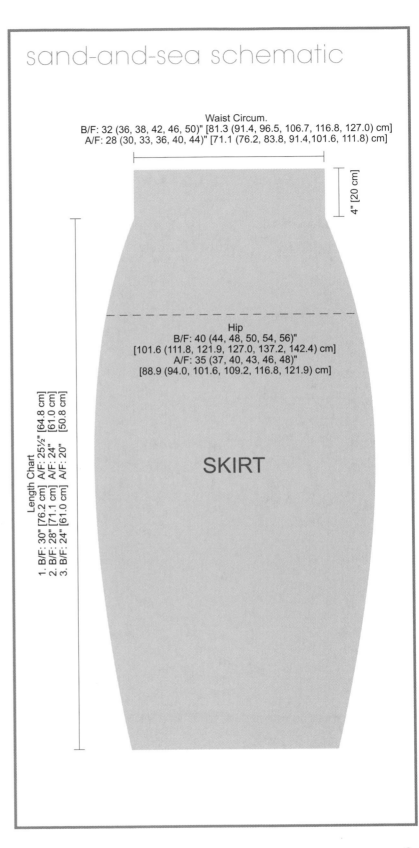

sand-and-sea schematic

Waist Circum.
B/F: 32 (36, 38, 42, 46, 50)" [81.3 (91.4, 96.5, 106.7, 116.8, 127.0) cm]
A/F: 28 (30, 33, 36, 40, 44)" [71.1 (76.2, 83.8, 91.4,101.6, 111.8) cm]

4" [20 cm]

Hip
B/F: 40 (44, 48, 50, 54, 56)"
[101.6 (111.8, 121.9, 127.0, 137.2, 142.4) cm]
A/F: 35 (37, 40, 43, 46, 48)"
[88.9 (94.0, 101.6, 109.2, 116.8, 121.9) cm]

SKIRT

Length Chart
1. B/F: 30" [76.2 cm]   A/F: 25½" [64.8 cm]
2. B/F: 28" [71.1 cm]   A/F: 24" [61.0 cm]
3. B/F: 24" [61.0 cm]   A/F: 20" [50.8 cm]

Victoria

Any fashion-conscious Victorian lady wouldn't dream of wearing a dress that did not have a lace collar adorning its neckline. In fact, as fashion changed over time, collars grew in size and drama—sometimes overtaking the wearer. This lacy neck scarf is reminiscent of the romance of that era; it features a ladder-style drape across the throat and shiny black buttons. Its subtle lace pattern softens after felting, making it very comfortable to wear.

skill level
Elementary

finished size*
(*completed scarf after felting)
• 15½" (39.4cm) around; one size fits most.

before-felting (B/F) measurements
• 16½" (41.9cm) circumference

materials
• Patons Classic Merino Wool: 100% pure wool (223 yds. (203.9m) / 3½ oz. (100g)), color #0026 Black, 1 skein

notions
• 4 buttons, each ⅜" (9mm), shank style
• Sewing thread (to match buttons)
• Hand-sewing needle

hooks
• H/8 (5.00mm), or size needed to obtain gauge

gauge
• 14 hdc and 11 rows = 4" (10.2cm) square before felting
• 14 hdc and 11 rows = 3¾" (9.5cm) square after felting

notes
• Strongly recommend hand-felting to control shrinkage.
• Collar is worked in one piece from end to end.
• Turning chain does not count as stitch unless otherwise noted.

abbreviations
See page 141.

Before Felting

After Felting

SPECIAL ABBREVIATIONS

6-ch-st (sextuple crochet): Yo 6 times, insert hook in next st, yo and pull up loop, (yo and pull through 2 loops 7 times)

5-ch-st (quintuple crochet): Yo 5 times, insert hook in next st, yo and pull up loop, (yo and pull through 2 loops 6 times)

4-ch-st (quadruple crochet): Yo 4 times, insert hook in next st, yo and pull up loop, (yo and pull through 2 loops 5 times)

3-ch-st (double-treble crochet): Yo 3 times, insert hook in next st, yo and pull up loop, (yo, draw through 2 loops 4 times)

STITCH PATTERN

(Worked over 10 sts)

Ch 7 (counts as first 6-ch-st), 6-ch-st in next st, 5-ch-st in next 2 sts, 4-ch-st in next 2 sts, 3-ch-st in next 2 sts, 2 dc in last 2 sts.

SCARF

Ch 21.

Row 1: Hdc in 2nd ch from hook, hdc across, turn (20 hdc).

Rows 2–5: Ch 1, hdc in each st across, turn.

Row 6: Work st pat over first 10 sts, hdc in each of last 10 sts, turn.

Rows 7–11: Work as for Row 2.

Rep Rows 6–11 five more times. **Note:** add or remove a rep to adjust the size.

Button Row: Ch 1, sc in each of next 2 sts, ch-3, sc in each of next 4 sts, ch-3, sc in each of next 5 sts, ch-3, sc in each of next 5 sts, ch-3, sc in each st to end. Fasten off.

FINISHING

Weave in all loose ends.

FELTING

See "Felting Basics" on pages 160 to 169. The scarf is soft-felted by hand. Check and measure your scarf frequently during the felting process. Felt and block the scarf to the finished-size measurements listed in the materials list, and let the scarf dry.

SEWING BUTTONS

Try on the scarf to ensure a comfortable fit, and align the loops on one side of the scarf to the button positions on the other. Use a hand-sewing needle and matching thread to sew on the buttons.

"Victoria" is a dramatic and demure scarf that draws attention to the face and neckline. Especially pretty when worn with a dress, the scarf is so versatile that it can be worn with a dressy coat, adding a suprising touch of elegance while keeping you warm.

Naturals & Neutrals

OCEAN, EARTH, AND SKY—THE COLORWAY OF THE PROJECTS IN THIS CHAPTER—EVOKE THE REASSURING BASICS OF LIFE IN HUES THAT INSTILL WARMTH AND COMFORT AND THAT HAVE A FAMILIAR, NATURAL FEEL. NEUTRAL TONES OFTEN REMIND US OF OUR SURROUNDINGS—BROWN IS THE COLOR OF THE EARTH AND BRICKS AND WOOD—THINGS THAT GIVE US A SENSE OF HOME AND COMFORT, SUCH AS OVEN-BAKED BREAD AND VELVETY CHOCOLATE. BLUE-GREEN IS THE COLOR OF NATURE—LEAVES, GRASS, AND WATER RUNNING OVER MOSS-COLORED ROCKS. NATURAL SHADES SUCH AS CREAM, WHITE, AND ECRU ARE THE COLORS OF SHEEP, RABBITS, AND OTHER ANIMALS THAT PROVIDE FLEECE THAT WILL BE SPUN AND WORKED BY HAND.

NATURAL AND NEUTRAL COLORS PLAY OUT IN THE ETHEREAL "LACEWING" WRAP MADE IN A LUSCIOUSLY SOFT ALPACA FIBER AND IN "SPANISH MOSS," A CAPELET WHOSE BLUE-GREEN AND BROWN TONES GROUND THE DESIGN. "CLEMATIS," A BROWN RAGLAN-SLEEVE SWEATER, SERVES AS A KIND OF "TRELLIS" FOR A FLORAL VINE, AND ORANGE APPEARS IN "LATTICE," A WOVEN MESSENGER BAG. GREENS AND WHITE FORM A PLAID FABRIC IN "ARAN," A SHOULDER BAG THAT USES A SPECIAL CROCHET TECHNIQUE TO REPRODUCE THE LOOK OF TRADITIONAL IRISH KNITTING. THE APPEAL OF NATURAL HUES IS APPARENT IN "CHOCOLATE VELVET," A TWIST-STYLE CAPELET; "JAMBIÈRES," LEG WARMERS; AND "ROCK CREEK," A V-NECK VEST IN A FLUFFY-MOHAIR BOUCLÉ THAT BRINGS WITH IT THE FEELING OF A FOREST, EVEN IF IT IS WORN IN THE URBAN "WILDS."

Clematis

THE TRAVELING VINES-AND-FLOWERS APPEAR TO EMERGE NATURALLY FROM THE BACK-GROUND OF THIS RAGLAN SWEATER, BUT THE DECORATION IS ACTUALLY AN APPLIQUÉ THAT IS FELTED AND ATTACHED SEPA-RATELY. THE PRETTY SWEATER IS WORKED IN THE ROUND FROM THE NECK TO THE WAIST IN ONE PIECE, ALLOWING YOU TO TRY ON THE SWEATER AS YOU WORK, ENSURING A PERFECT FIT.

Before Felting

After Felting

skill level

Intermediate

finished size*

(*completed sweater after felting, blocking, assembling)
- **Small:** 34" (86.4cm) bust and 20" (50.8cm) long
- **Medium:** 38" (76.5cm) bust and 20" (50.8cm) long
- **Large:** 42" (106.5cm) bust and 20" (50.8cm) long
- **X-Large:** 46" (116.8cm) bust and 20" (50.8cm) long

before-felting (B/F) and after-felting (A/F) measurements

See schematic.

materials

- MC: Berroco Ultra Alpaca; 50% alpaca, 50% wool (216 yds. (197.5m) 3½ oz. / (100g)), color #6280, 5 (5, 6, 6) skeins
- CC1: Blue Sky Alpacas Melange; 100% baby alpaca (110 yds. (100.5m) / 1¾ oz. (50g)), color #800 Cornflower, 1 skein
- CC2: Blue Sky Alpacas Sport Weight; 100% baby alpaca (110 yds. (100.5m) / 1¾ oz. (50g)), color #500 Natural White, 1 skein

notions

- 12 round beads, 4mm (for center of flower)
- Hand-sewing needle
- Sewing threads to match flower, leaves, and stems
- Tapestry needle
- Removable stitch markers

hooks

- G/6 (4.25mm), or size needed to obtain gauge
- H/8 (5.00mm), or size needed to obtain gauge
- K/11 (6.50mm), or size needed to obtain gauge

gauge

- 14 hdc and 12 rows = 4" (10.2cm) using small hook and MC before felting
- 12 hdc and 10 rows = 4" (10.2cm) using medium hook and CC1 or CC2 before felting
- 12 hdc and 10 rows = 3" (7.6cm) using large hook and CC1 or CC2 after felting

notes

- Sweater is not felted.
- Sweater is worked in rounds, start-ing at neck edge.
- Turning chain does not count as stitch.
- Appliqué pieces are cut from felted fabric and sewn onto sweater.

abbreviations

See page 141.

Clematis

SWEATER

With smaller hook and MC, ch 72 (80, 88, 96) loosely, sl st in first ch to form ring, being careful not to twist yarn.

Rnd 1: Ch 1, hdc in first ch and in each ch around, join with sl st in first ch (72, (80, 88, 96) hdc).

Rnd 2: (Raglan Setup Row) Ch 1, * work 16 (18, 20, 22) hdc, 2hdc in next st, pm in st just made, work 2 hdc in next st, rep from * 3 more times, (4 markers placed), join with sl st in first st.

Rnd 3: Ch 1, * hdc to one st before marker, 2 hdc in next st, move marker to st just made, 2 hdc in next st, rep from * 3 more times, join with sl st in first st.

Rep Rnd 3 until you have 40 (42, 44, 46) sts between each set of markers.

Rnd 4: Ch 1, * hdc to marker, move marker to st just made, 2 hdc in next st, hdc to 1 st before marker, 2 hdc in next st, move marker to st just made, rep from * once more, join with sl st in first st.

Rep Rnd 4 until you have 60 (68, 74, 80) hdc for Front and Back and still have 40 (42, 44, 46) sts at each sleeve. Continue in even rounds of hdc until yoke measures approx. 7 (8, 8½, 9)" (17.8 (20.3, 21.6, 22.9) cm) or desired length from neckline, ending just before one of the markers at beginning of Back or Front. **Note:** try on the sweater for size; the sleeve portions should wrap comfortably around your arms.

(continued on page 98)

clematis schematic

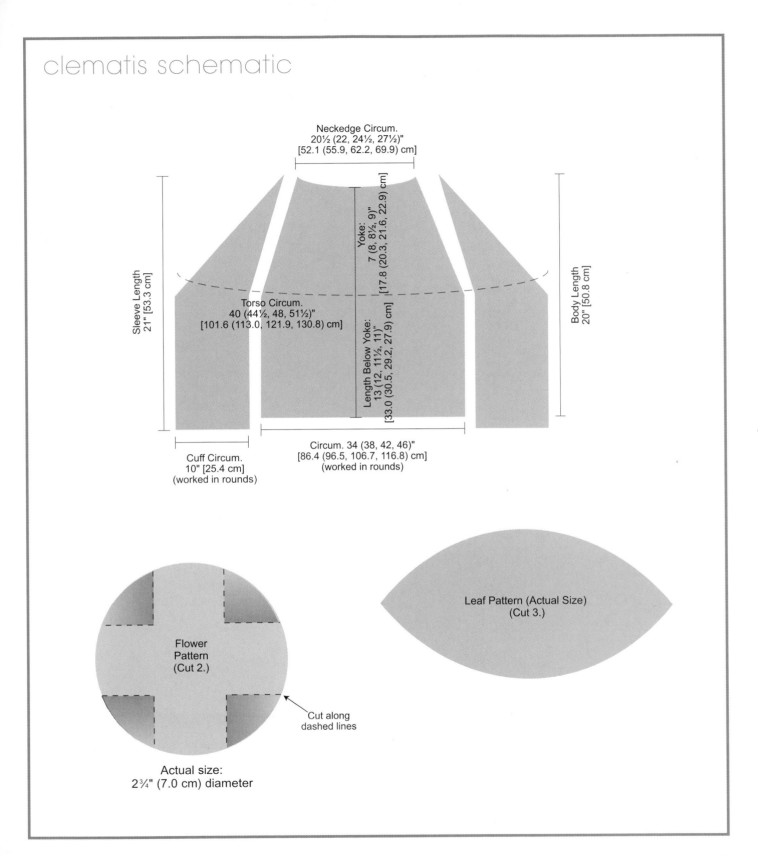

Neckedge Circum.
20½ (22, 24½, 27½)"
[52.1 (55.9, 62.2, 69.9) cm]

Yoke:
7 (8, 8½, 9)"
[17.8 (20.3, 21.6, 22.9) cm]

Sleeve Length
21" [53.3 cm]

Torso Circum.
40 (44½, 48, 51½)"
[101.6 (113.0, 121.9, 130.8) cm]

Length Below Yoke:
13 (12, 11½, 11)"
[33.0 (30.5, 29.2, 27.9) cm]

Body Length
20" [50.8 cm]

Cuff Circum.
10" [25.4 cm]
(worked in rounds)

Circum. 34 (38, 42, 46)"
[86.4 (96.5, 106.7, 116.8) cm]
(worked in rounds)

Flower
Pattern
(Cut 2.)

Cut along
dashed lines

Actual size:
2¾" (7.0 cm) diameter

Leaf Pattern (Actual Size)
(Cut 3.)

Clematis

(continued from page 96)

BODY

Rnd 1: Ch 1, * hdc to marker, remove marker, ch 10, skip next 40 (42, 44, 46) sts, remove next marker, rep from * once more. **Note:** you should have 140 (156, 168, 180) sts for the body of the garment.
Continue in even rounds of hdc, working 1 hdc into each ch at underarms until body measures 20" (50.8cm) from neckline or desired length. **Note:** try on the sweater for size.
Fasten off.

SLEEVES

Rnd 1: Join yarn with sl st to first Sleeve, work 1 rnd even hdc around sleeve sts and Back of ch-10 from Body, placing marker at center of underarm, join with sl st.
Rnd 2: Ch 1, hdc around, join with sl st.

Begin sleeve decreases

Rnd 1: Ch 1, hdc to st before marker, remove marker, hdc2tog over next 2 sts, replace marker in st just made, hdc to end of round, join with sl st.
Rnds 2–3: Ch-1, hdc around, join with sl st.

Rep. Rnds 1–3 until Sleeve circumference is 10" (25.4cm), or desired width. Work even until Sleeve measures 21" (53.3cm) in length. Repeat for second Sleeve.

FLOWER

Note: two sections of the flower are cut from the crocheted fabric made using this pattern:
With medium hook and CC2 (white), ch 31.
Row 1: Hdc in second ch from hook and in each ch across, turn.
Row 2: Ch 1, hdc across, turn.
Rep Row 2 until piece measures 12" (30.5cm).
Fasten off.

LEAVES

Note: three leaves are cut from the crocheted fabric made using this patttern:
With medium hook and CC2 (blue), ch 31.
Row 1: Hdc in second ch from hook and in each ch across, turn.
Row 2: Ch 1, hdc across, turn.
Rep Row 2 until piece measures 12" (30.5cm).
Fasten off.

STEMS

(Make 3.)
With two strands of CC1 (blue) held together and large hook, ch 30. Fasten off.

FINISHING

Note: the sweater is NOT felted.

FELTING THE LEAF, FLOWER, AND STEM

See "Felting Basics" on pages 160 to169. The fabric for the flower and leaves, and the chain for the stems are hand-felted. Felt and block the fabrics, and lay them flat to dry.

MAKING THE FLOWER

Enlarge and copy the pattern on page 97 so that the diameter of the circle is 2¾" (7.0cm). Use the pattern to cut out two flower layers. Stack the layers, and sew on the beads to the center. Set aside.

MAKING THE LEAVES

Copy the actual-size pattern on page 97, and make three leaves, each measuring 3" (7.6cm) from tip to tip. Position and sew the flower, leaves, and stems to the sweater using the photograph as a guide.

Crocheting a sweater "top~down" allows you to adjust the fit of your sweater by working fewer (or more) raglan increases; you can adjust the length of the sweater and sleeves with no fancy figuring~ just crochet until the sweater fits as desired.

Lacewing

THE LACEWING MOTH HAS BEAUTIFUL FILI-GREED WINGS THAT ALLOW LIGHT TO FILTER THROUGH THEM. THIS FEATURE IS MOST IMPOR-TANT IN ANOTHER WAY—IT MAKES THE MOTH'S DELICATE WINGS ALMOST WEIGHTLESS, ALLOW-ING IT TO FLY. HERE, AN EASY AND FAST VICTORIAN NEEDLEWORK TECHNIQUE CALLED HAIRPIN LACE IS USED TO CREATE THE LACY FABRIC FOR "LACEWING." MADE FROM INCREDI-BLY SOFT BRUSHED SURI ALPACA, THE LUXURI-OUS ACCESSORY IS LIGHTWEIGHT AND COZY TO WEAR AS A SCARF OR A SHAWL.

skill level
Elementary

finished size*
(*completed scarf/shawl after assembling the lace strips and felting them)
- 18" (45.7cm) wide and 60" (152.4cm) long, exclusive of fringe

before-felting (BF) measurements
- 24" (61.0cm) wide and 80" (203.2cm) long

materials
- BMC: Blue Sky Alpacas Brushed Suri; 67% baby suri, 22% Merino, 11% bamboo (142 yd. (129.8 m) / 1¾ oz. (50 g)), color #900, 6 skeins

notions
- Hairpin-lace frame
- Safety pin

hook
- N/13 (9.00 mm), or size needed to obtain gauge

gauge
- Gauge is determined by the width of the space between the prongs of the hairpin-lace frame.

notes
- Scarf/shawl is made up of multiple strips of hairpin lace that are crocheted together.
- Scarf/shawl is soft-felted.
- Caution: alpaca yarn felts very quickly—in approx. 20 seconds—so hand-felting is recommended.

abbreviations
See page 141.

Before Felting

After Felting

SPECIAL TECHNIQUE: HAIRPIN LACE

Hairpin lace is a style of crochet that is worked on a hairpin-lace frame using a crochet hook. The frame has two rods called prongs that are held apart by cross bars; the space between the prongs determines the width of the strip of lace that is produced. Hairpin-lace frames are available in a variety of widths; most are adjustable. To create hairpin-lace fabric, yarn is wrapped around the prongs of the frame in a criss-cross pattern and crocheted up the center using a crochet hook. The line of crochet stitches at the center is called the spine.

SHAWL/SCARF
HAIRPIN-LACE STRIP
(Make 6.)
Set Up the Frame
Adjust the metal prongs on the frame to 2½" (6.4cm) apart.

ATTACHING SCRAP YARN

Measure and cut a 40" length (101.6 cm) of contrasting scrap yarn. Attach the ends of the scrap yarn to the top bar of the frame where it intersects each prong. **Note:** the scrap yarn forms a U-shape that hangs down alongside the prongs. As you work, you'll be wrapping the yarn around the scrap yarn *and* the prongs of the frame so that when you remove the hairpin-lace strip, the scrap yarn will be threaded through the loops of the strip, keeping them in good order. As the work becomes longer than the prongs, allow it to fall off of the prongs and onto the scrap yarn. Roll the strip as you go, securing it with a safety pin.

HAIRPIN-LACE STRIP (Make 6.)
Step 1: Using two strands of MC held together, attach the yarn with a slip knot around the left prong.

Step 2: Wrap the yarn from front to back over the right prong. **Note:** yarn is now at the back of the frame.

Step3: Insert the hook up throuh the left loop, yo, and pull through, yo and pull through both loops on the hook (sc).

Step 4: With the loop still on the hook, bring the hook through the frame to the back of the work.

Step 5: Flip the frame from left to right, allowing the yarn to wrap around what was the left prong. **Note:** the hook should now be in the front of the work. Rep steps 4 and 5 to make one strip.

Rep the steps to make one strip with 120 loops on each prong of the frame; then slide all of the loops onto the scrap yarn, and secure them with a safety pin until you're ready to join the strips together.

Cont until there is a total of 6 strips.

JOINING THE STRIPS

Insert the hook into one loop of one strip, then into one loop of a second strip.

Draw the second loop through the first. With the second loop still on the hook, insert the hook in the next loop up on the first strip.

Keep moving back and forth until you've joined two strips by their loops along their full lengths.

Join the next strip to one open side of the loops of a third strip.

Repeat until all the strips are joined together.

FINISHING
Weave in all ends.

FELTING
See "Felting Basics" on pages 160 to 169. The shawl is just *slightly* soft-felted; it is only kept in hot water for 20 seconds. Felt and block the scarf/shawl, and lay it flat to dry.

ADDING FRINGE

Measure and cut four 20" (50.8cm) strands for each fringe. Attach the fringe with a lark's-head knot (a.k.a. cow hitch). Fold the group of four strands of yarn in half; pass the folded end through a space in the edge of the shawl; and pull the ends through the loop to secure the fringe. Repeat evenly across both ends of the scarf/shawl as shown.

Hairpin lace is going through a resurgence in popularity because it is not only a simple and fun needlework, but it takes little time to do. To make fabric with an elegant look and feel, choose alpaca, Merino, and mohair yarns.

Lattice

Bags are the ultimate accessory—you can't have too many of them. Whether one is large or small, a bag can add style to an outfit and hold what you need at the same time. "Lattice" is an adorable messenger-style bag in rich burnt orange. Created with simple strips of crocheted fabric that are woven together, the bag features braided tab closures with round hoop-shaped pewter buckles. Once you learn the easy weaving technique, you can use it to make other accessories, such as rugs, placemats, and pillows.

skill level

Intermediate

finished size*

(*completed bag after felting and assembling)
- 12" (30.5cm) wide and 12" (30.5cm) tall with a 5" long (12.7cm) flap

before-felting (B/F) measurements

- Short strip: 1¼" (3.2cm) wide and 17" (43.2cm) long
- Long strip: 1¼" (3.2cm) wide and 44" (111.8cm) long
- Strap: 4" (3.2cm) wide and 60" (152.4cm) long

materials

- Vermont Organic Fiber Company O-Wool: 100% organic merino wool (198 yds. (178.2m) / 3½ oz. (100g)), color Saffron, 3 skeins

notions

- Sturdy fabric, approx. 12" x 20" (30.5cm x 50.8cm) (for lining*)
  *Note: canvas, leather, or vinyl are good fabric choices.
- 2 buckles as desired
- Permanent fabric adhesive
- Upholstery thread
- Needles: upholstery; tapestry
- Towel, 14" x 20" (35.6cm x 50.8cm)
- Pins: straight or safety

hooks

- H/8 (5.00mm), or size needed to obtain gauge

gauge

- 12 hdc and 10 rows = 4" (10.2cm) before felting
- 12 hdc and 10 rows = 3" (7.6cm) after felting

1 strip made of 4 hdc = 1¼" (3.2cm) wide before felting and ¾" (1.9cm) after felting

notes

- Bag is created from crocheted strips of hdc that are felted before they are woven together.
- Turning chain does not count as stitch.

abbreviations

See page 141.

Before Felting

After Felting

Lattice

Row 2: Ch 1, hdc across, turn.
Repeat Row 2 until 150 rows have been worked from beg. **Note:** piece should measure approx. 60" (152.4cm).
Fasten off.

FINISHING
FELTING
See "Felting Basics" on pages 160 to 169. Felt the strips until the short strips measure 12½" (31.8cm), the long strips measure 33" (83.8cm), and the strip for the handle strap measures approx. 45" (1.1m). Lay the strips flat to dry, using pins at the edges to ensure even shaping.

ASSEMBLING
Note: the long strips will be the warp of the woven bag and will lay in a horizontal orientation; the short strips will be the weft and will lay in a vertical orientation.

Lay the long strips parallel with one another in a horizontal orientation on a towel; pin along the top and bottom edges of each strip.

BAG
SHORT STRIP
(Make 38.)
Ch 5.
Row 1: Hdc in 2nd ch from hook and in ch across, turn (4 hdc).
Row 2: Ch 1, hdc in each st across, turn.
Repeat Row 2 until 42 rows have been worked from beg. **Note:** pieces should measure approx. 17" (43.2cm).
Fasten off.

LONG STRIP
(Make 11.)
Work as for Short Strip until 110 rows have been worked from beg. **Note:** piece should measure approx. 44" (111.8cm).
Fasten off.

HANDLE STRAP
Ch 13.
Row 1: Hdc in second ch from hook and in ch across, turn (12 hdc).

HELPFUL TIP
"Lattice" is a great portable project—the strips are narrow and use only a few yards of yarn each. For a fun twist, make "Lattice" in a mixed-color pattern using scraps of yarn from other projects. You can design your bag in advance by laying out lengths of yarn and experimenting with different color combinations.

Beginning at the top strip, weave a short strip over and under each long strip, letting any excess length extend beyond the bottom edge of the weaving.

Repeat until all the short strips are used. **Note:** what's left of the long (warp) strips becomes the tab closures and the hem for the flap.

Hand-sew long running sts along the outer strips on all four sides of the weaving to keep the strips in place. (You'll undo these sts later.) Fold the weaving to make a bag whose pouch measures 12" deep (30.5cm), base measures 3" wide (7.6cm), and flap measures 5" long (12.7cm).

Pin one edge of each end of the handle strap to the base of the bag at each side, pinning the side edges of the strip to opposite edges of the bag's sides. Hand-sew the strap to the bag.

BRAIDED TABS
Use the rem length of the long strips at the flap edge of the bag, skipping 1 long strip, braiding the next 3 strips, skipping the next 3 long strips, and braiding the next 3 strips. With the 3 ends of braided strips layered tog into a point, hand-sew the point of braid together to secure.

Fold the remaining single long strips to the wrong side of the flap; then trim the rem strips to 1" (2.5cm), and sew them to the inside of the flap.

LINING
Measure the bag's interior, including the flap, and cut a rectangle of lining fabric to that measurement, adding 2" (5.0cm) to the length and the width. Fold over and press a ¾" (1.9cm) hem along all four sides of the rectangle. Put the lining into the bag, right side out, matching the folded hems of the lining to the side edges of the bag and the flap. Smooth the lining along the front, across the bottom, and up and along the front flap of the bag. Glue the lining fabric in place along its hemmed edges. After the glue has dried completely, remove the basting stitches in the weaving (made in the Assembling step.) Hand-sew around the bag opening and the flap to secure the lining.

ACCENT BUCKLES
Hand-sew the buckles to the bag as shown, using a threaded needle.

Spanish Moss

In oak groves in the South, brown Spanish moss and lush green leaves can be so thick that if you are standing underneath a tree, the sky might be completely obscured except for bits of blue that peek through. The subtle stripes in this capelet and the bouclé effect (produced by felting) evoke the same soft colors of a tree-filled Southern landscape. The capelet has flared sleeves and uses an innovative one-piece construction to achieve the look of a cape and a jacket.

Before Felting

After Felting

skill level

Intermediate

finished size*

*Completed capelet after felting, blocking, assembling, and finishing
- **Small:** 36" (91.4cm) bust and 16" (40.6cm) long
- **Medium:** 38" (96.5 cm) bust and 16" (40.6 cm) long
- **Large:** 42" (106.7 cm) bust and 21" (53.3cm) long
- **X-Large:** 46" (116.8 cm) bust and 21" (53.3 cm) long

before-felting (B/F) and after-felting (A/F) measurements

See schematic.

materials

- Di.ve' Autunno: 100% Merino (98 yds. (89.6 m) / 1¾ oz. (50 g)), color #32965, 14 (16, 18, 20) skeins

notions

- Tapestry needle

hooks

- US J/10 (6.00mm), or size needed to obtain gauge

gauge

- 10 hdc and 8 rows = 4" (10.2 cm) square before felting
- 10 hdc and 8 rows = 3" (7.6cm) square after felting

notes

- Capelet is worked in one piece from neck down using raglan shaping.
- Turning chain does not count as stitch.

abbreviations

See page 141.

Spanish Moss

SPECIAL ABBREVIATIONS
V-st: (hdc, ch 1, hdc) all in same st or ch-sp indicated.

CAPELET
Ch 88 (93 98, 101).
Row 1: Hdc in second ch from hook and in each ch across. Turn 87 (92, 97, 100) hdc.

SET UP FOR RAGLAN INC.
Row 1: Ch1, hdc in each of first 20 (21, 22, 22) hdc to form right Front. V-st in next st, hdc in each of next 14 (15, 16, 17) hdc to form right Sleeve. V-st in next st, hdc in each of next 14 (15, 16, 17) hdc to form back. V-st in next st, hdc in each of next 14 (15, 16, 17) hdc to form left Sleeve. V-st in next st, hdc in each of next 21 (22, 23, 23) hdc to form left Front, turn.

Row 2: Ch1, hdc across, working in V-st in each ch-1 sp on previous row.
Rep Row 2 until fabric measures 12 (12, 16, 16)" (30.5 (30.5, 40.6, 40.6) cm) from beg.

FRONT
Ch 1, hdc across to first ch-1, turn. Cont working in hdc over just these Front sts until piece measures 21 (21, 28, 28)" (53.3 (53.3, 71.1, 71.1) cm) from foundation row. Fasten off.

SLEEVE
Using sl st, skip ch-1 sp and attach yarn to next hdc. Ch 1, hdc across to next ch-1 sp, turn.
Cont to work even in hdc over these Sleeve sts until piece measures 21 (21, 28, 28)" (53.3 (53.3, 71.1, 71.1) cm) from foundation row. Fasten off.

Work as directed above for the Back, second Sleeve, and second Front. **Note:** make sure all pieces are the same length when measured from the neck edge.

COLLAR
Ch 61(61, 66, 66).
Row 1: Hdc in 2nd ch from hook and each ch across, turn (60 (60, 65, 65) hdc).
Row 2: Ch 1, hdc across, turn.
Rep Row 2 until piece measures 4" (10.2cm) from beginning. Fasten off.

FINISHING
FELTING
See "Felting Basics" on pages 160 to 169. The cape and collar are soft-felted. Felt the sections to the after-felting (A/F) measurements listed in the schematic. Check and measure the pieces frequently during the felting process. Block the pieces, and let them dry.

ASSEMBLING
Sew the side seams. Sew the sleeve seams if desired, leaving at least a 6" (15.2cm) opening at the edge of the Sleeve.

Fold the Collar in half, and mark the center point using a pin. Mark the center back of the neck opening using a pin. With the right sides together, pin the Collar to the neck at the marked points, and ease the Collar into the neck opening until it fits. Pin the collar in place, and sew the collar to the neck opening.

Spanish moss schematic

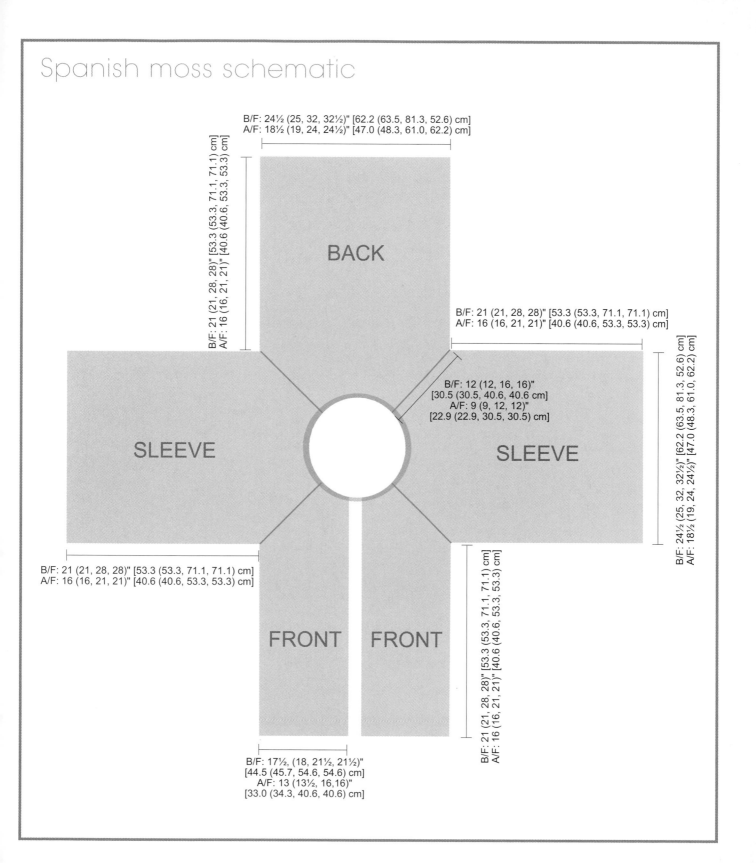

B/F: 24½ (25, 32, 32½)" [62.2 (63.5, 81.3, 52.6) cm]
A/F: 18½ (19, 24, 24½)" [47.0 (48.3, 61.0, 62.2) cm]

B/F: 21 (21, 28, 28)" [53.3 (53.3, 71.1, 71.1) cm]
A/F: 16 (16, 21, 21)" [40.6 (40.6, 53.3, 53.3) cm]

BACK

B/F: 21 (21, 28, 28)" [53.3 (53.3, 71.1, 71.1) cm]
A/F: 16 (16, 21, 21)" [40.6 (40.6, 53.3, 53.3) cm]

B/F: 12 (12, 16, 16)"
[30.5 (30.5, 40.6, 40.6 cm]
A/F: 9 (9, 12, 12)"
[22.9 (22.9, 30.5, 30.5) cm]

SLEEVE

SLEEVE

B/F: 24½ (25, 32, 32½)" [62.2 (63.5, 81.3, 52.6) cm]
A/F: 18½ (19, 24, 24½)" [47.0 (48.3, 61.0, 62.2) cm]

B/F: 21 (21, 28, 28)" [53.3 (53.3, 71.1, 71.1) cm]
A/F: 16 (16, 21, 21)" [40.6 (40.6, 53.3, 53.3) cm]

FRONT FRONT

B/F: 21 (21, 28, 28)" [53.3 (53.3, 71.1, 71.1) cm]
A/F: 16 (16, 21, 21)" [40.6 (40.6, 53.3, 53.3) cm]

B/F: 17½, (18, 21½, 21½)"
[44.5 (45.7, 54.6, 54.6) cm]
A/F: 13 (13½, 16,16)"
[33.0 (34.3, 40.6, 40.6) cm]

Rock Creek

THE STEELY-BLUE, SANDY-BEIGE, AND GREEN-GREY COLORS IN THIS MOHAIR BOUCLÉ FABRIC ARE REMINISCENT OF WATER RUSHING OVER STONES IN A CREEK BED. WHAT BETTER ACCESSORY FOR A WALK ALONG A RIVER THAN THIS FASHIONABLY OVERSIZED VEST? THE TUNIC LENGTH AND V-NECK SHAPING GIVE THE VEST A FLATTERING FIT, WHILE THE OVERSIZED SCARF-LIKE COLLAR ADDS WARMTH AND VISUAL INTEREST. THIS VEST IS ONLY LIGHTLY FELTED, LEAVING A SOFT FABRIC THAT IS TRUE TO THE TEXTURE OF NATURAL MOHAIR.

Before Felting

After Felting

skill level

Intermediate

finished size*

(*completed vest after felting and finishing)
- **Small/Medium:** 44" (111.8cm) bust and 26" (66.0cm) long from the shoulder
- **Large/X-Large:** 52" (132.1cm) bust and 26" (66.0cm) long from the shoulder

before-felting (B/F) and after-felting (A/F) measurements

See schematic.

materials

- Be Sweet Boucle Mohair: 100% baby mohair (120 yds. (109.7m) / 1³/₄ oz. (50g)), color Slate, 10 (12) skeins

notions

- Tapestry needle
- 1 yd. (0.9m) suede lacing, ³/₁₆" (0.5cm) wide

hooks

- J/10 (6.00mm), or size needed to obtain gauge

gauge

- 10 hdc and 8 rows = 4" (10.2cm) before felting
- 10 hdc and 8 rows = 3¹/₂" (8.9cm) after felting

notes

- Turning ch does not count as stitch unless otherwise noted.

abbreviations

See page 141.

Rock Creek

SPECIAL ABBREVIATIONS

Hdc2tog: Yo, insert hook in next st, yo and draw up a loop twice, yo and draw through all 5 loops on hook.

VEST
BACK
Ch 56 (66).

Row 1: Hdc in second ch from hook and each ch across, turn (55 (65) hdc).

Row 2: Ch 1, hdc across, turn.

Rep Row 2 until 48 rows have been worked from beg.

Note: piece should measure approx. 24" (61.0cm) from foundation row.

BEGIN NECK SHAPING FOR RIGHT SHOULDER
Row 1 (RS): Ch 1, work 17 (18) hdc, hdc2tog, turn (18 (19) hdc).

Row 2 (WS): Ch 1, hdc across, turn.

Repeat last two rows until 15 hdc remain.

Fasten off.

LEFT SHOULDER
With WS facing, reattach yarn with sl st to outside edge. Work as for right shoulder.

FRONT
(Make 2.)

Ch 28 (33).

Row 1: Hdc in second ch from hook and each ch across, turn (27 (32) hdc).

Row 2: Ch 1, hdc across, turn.

Rep Row 2 until 24 rows have been worked from beg.

Note: piece should measure approx. 12" (30.5cm).

BEGIN NECK SHAPING

Row 1: Ch 1, hdc to last 2 sts, hdc2tog, turn (26 (31) hdc).

Row 2: Ch 1, hdc across, turn.

Rep last two rows until 15 hdc remain, then work even in rows of hdc until piece measures 26" (66.0cm) from beg of piece.

Fasten off.

COLLAR

Ch 21(26).

Row 1: Hdc in second ch from hook and each ch across, turn (20 (25) hdc).

Row 2: Ch 1, hdc across, turn.

Rep Row 2 until piece measures 50" (127.0cm) from foundation row.

Fasten off.

FELTING

See "Felting Basics" on pages 160 to 169. Pieces are soft-felted. Felt and check pieces to the after-felting (A/F) measurements listed in the schematic. Block the pieces, and lay them flat to dry.

(continued on page 116)

HELPFUL TIP

Felting will significantly change the look of the crocheted fabric, especially if you crochet with a "hairy" yarn, such as 100-percent alpaca, cashmere, or mohair. These tend to felt quickly. To ensure good results, stay near your washing machine as you work or use hand-felting.

Rock Creek

(continued from page 115)

SHOULDER AND SIDE SEAMS

Join Front and Back at shoulders. Sew side seams.

ATTACH COLLAR

Locate and mark the center of the back neck opening. Mark the center of Collar, and pin the marked points together. Then stretch the Collar to fit it along the neckline, and pin it in place. Sew the Collar to the neck opening.

EDGING

Sc around all of the edges, including armholes.

RIBBON CLOSURE

Cut the suede ribbon in half.
Fold one piece in half, and thread the folded loop through the first front edge at the point where the neck shaping begins. Pull two ends of the ribbon through the loop, and tighten as if making a fringe. Rep on the second front edge.

rock-creek schematic

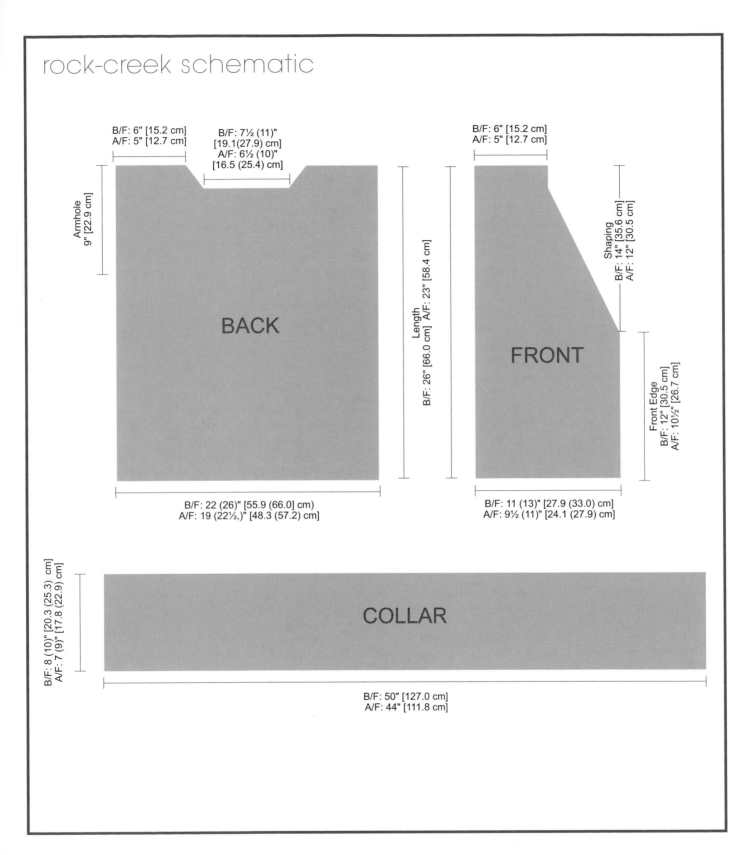

BACK

B/F: 6" [15.2 cm]
A/F: 5" [12.7 cm]

B/F: 7½ (11)"
[19.1(27.9) cm]
A/F: 6½ (10)"
[16.5 (25.4) cm]

Armhole
9" [22.9 cm]

B/F: 22 (26)" [55.9 (66.0) cm]
A/F: 19 (22½,)" [48.3 (57.2) cm]

Length
B/F: 26" [66.0 cm] A/F: 23" [58.4 cm]

FRONT

B/F: 6" [15.2 cm]
A/F: 5" [12.7 cm]

Shaping
B/F: 14" [35.6 cm]
A/F: 12" [30.5 cm]

Front Edge
B/F: 12" [30.5 cm]
A/F: 10½" [26.7 cm]

B/F: 11 (13)" [27.9 (33.0) cm]
A/F: 9½ (11)" [24.1 (27.9) cm]

COLLAR

B/F: 8 (10)" [20.3 (25.3) cm]
A/F: 7 (9)" [17.8 (22.9) cm]

B/F: 50" [127.0 cm]
A/F: 44" [111.8 cm]

Aran

Traditional Aran knitting, which arrived in Ireland in the early 1900s, uses complex stitches to create intricate and lyrical patterns—similar to the ancient Irish symbols seen on old stone carvings. Here, our "Aran" bag, complete with hoop-shaped handles in soft yellow, uses crochet stitches called "post stitches" to mimic the look of traditional Irish knitting.

Before Felting

After Felting

skill level

Advanced

finished size*

(*completed bag after felting)
- 33" (83.8cm) circumference and 18" (45.7cm) tall

before-felting (B/F) measurements

- 38" (96.5cm) circumference and 20" (50.8cm) tall

materials

- Patons Classic Merino Wool: 100% wool (223 yds. (203.9m) / 3½ oz. (100g)), color #00229 Natural Mix, 3 skeins

notions

- Stitch markers
- Tapestry needle
- Sheet of plastic canvas (for reinforcement)
- Chalk (for tracing)
- ½ yd. (45.7cm) fabric (for lining)
- Sewing thread (to match lining)
- Hand-sewing needle
- 2 bamboo purse rings, each 6" (15.2cm) circumference
- Permanent adhesive

hook

- H/8 (5.00mm), or size needed to obtain gauge

gauge

- 14 hdc and 11 rows = 4" (10.2cm) square before felting
- 14 hdc and 11 rows = 3½" (8.9cm) square after felting

notes

- Base of bag is worked in spiral without joining rounds: use stitch marker in first st to keep track of rounds.
- When you begin to work cable patterns, place stitch markers between each pattern section to keep track of patterns.
- Front Post treble crochet (FPtr) is worked around post of specified stitch two rows below working row. (When post stitches are worked, there tends to be a gap behind the stitch. To reduce the gap effect, work the post stitch until there are 2 loops left on the hook; then work hdc in the next stitch of the working row; and finish off the post stitch.)
- Turning chain does not count as stitch.

abbreviations

See page 141.

special abbreviations

V-stitch (V-st): (Hdc, ch 1, hdc) all in one ch-sp.

FPtr (Front Post treble): Yo twice, insert hook from front to back and around the post of stitch indicated, yo, pull up loop, (yo, pull through 2 loops on hook) two times, yo, insert hook in next st of working row (behind post stitch), yo, pull up a loop, yo, pull through 3 loops on hook, yo, pull through 2 loops on hook.

Aran

STITCH PATTERN 1 (st pat 1)
(Worked over 15 sts)

Rnd 1: Sk next 2 sts, FPtr around post of next st 2 rnds below, hdc in next st, Fptr in first skipped st from 2 rnds below (crossing in front of last FPtr), *hdc in each of next 3 sts, sk next 2 sts, FPtr around post of next st 2 rnds below, hdc in next st, FPtr in first skipped st from 2 rnds below (crossing in front of last FPtr. Rep from * once.

Rnd 2: Hdc in each st across.

Rnd 3: FPtr around first FPtr from 2 rnds below, hdc in next hdc, FPtr around next FPtr, *hdc in each of next 3 hdc, FPtr around next FPtr, hdc in next hdc, FPtr around next FPtr; rep from * once.

Rnd 4: Rep Rnd 2.

Rnd 5: Sk first FPtr from 2 rnds below, FPtr around post of next FPtr, hdc in next st, Fptr in first skipped FPtr from 2 rnds below (crossing in front of last FPtr), *hdc in each of next 3 sts, sk next FPtr from 2 rnds below, FPtr around post of next FPtr, hdc in next st, Fptr in last skipped FPtr from 2 rnds below (crossing in front of last FPtr); rep from * once.

Rep rounds 2–5 for pattern.

STITCH PATTERN 2 (st pat 2)
(Worked over 6 sts)

Rnd 1: (FPtr around post of next st from 2 rnds below) 6 times.

Rnd 2: Hdc in each st across.

Rnds 3: (FPtr around post of next FPtr from 2 rnds below) 6 times.

Rnd 4: Rep Rnd 2.

Rnds 5–6: Rep Rnds 3 and 4.

Rnd 7: Hdc in each of next 2 hdc, leaving last loop of each st on hook work FPtr Cl as follows: FPtr around each FPtr from 2 rnds below, yo, pull through 7 loops on hook, ch 1 (does not count as st), hdc in each of next 3 hdc.

Rnd 8: Rep Rnd 2.

Rnd 9: Working each st around post of ch-1 st from FPtr Cl below, FPtr in each of next 6 sts.

Rnd 10: Rep Rnd 2.

Rnd 11: (FPtr around post of next FPtr from 2 rnds below) 6 times. Rep rnds 2–11 for patt.

STITCH PATTERN 3 (st pat 3)
(Worked over 7 sts)

Rnd 1: Hdc in next st, sk next 2 sts, FPtr around post of next st 2 rnds below, hdc in next st, FPtr in around same st as previous FPtr, hdc in next st, FPtr around same st as previous FPtr, hdc in next st.

Rnd 2: Hdc in each st across.

Rnd 3: FPtr around first FPtr from 2 rnds below, *hdc in each of next 2 sts, FPtr in next FPtr from 2 rnds below; rep from * once.

Rnd 4: Rep Rnd 2.

Rnd 5: *Hdc in next st, FPtr around post of second FPtr (center FPtr) from 2 rnds below; rep from * twice, hdc in next st.

Rnds 6–10: Rep Rnds 2–5, then rep Rnd 2 once more.

Rnd 11: Hdc in each of next 3 hdc, FPtr around second FPtr (center FPtr) from 2 rnds below, hdc in each of next 3 hdc.

Rnd 12: Rep Rnd 2.

Rnd 13: Rep Rnd 11.

Rnds 14–17: Rep Rnd 2.

Rep rnds 1–17 for pat.

BAG

Bag is worked in rounds from the bottom up.

BASE

Ch 22.

Rnd 1: Work 3 hdc in second ch from hook, hdc in each of next 19 ch, 3 hdc in last ch. **Note:** rotate the work so you can now begin working across the bottom loops of the foundation chain, hdc in next 19 ch, join with sl st in first st (44 hdc).

Rnd 2: Ch 1, V-st in first st, *hdc in next st, V-st in next st; hdc in next 19 sts*, V-st in next st; rep from * to * once, do not join (48 hdc).

Rnd 3: Hdc in each st around working V-st in each ch-1 sp; do not join (56 hdc). Rep Rnd 3 working in a spiral without joining, until you have 128 hdc, sl st in next st. Fasten off.

BODY

Locate the 3 centermost sts on one side of bag, and join yarn with sl st in first of 3 sts; ch 1, hdc in each hdc and ch-1 sp around, join with sl st in first st (132 hdc).
Next rnd: Ch 1, hdc in each st around, join with sl st in first st to join.

BEGIN CABLE PATTERNS

*Work st pat 1 over first 15 sts, hdc in next 5 sts, work st pat 2 over next 6 sts, hdc in next 5 sts, work st pat 3 over next 7 sts, hdc in next 5 sts, work st pat 2 over next 6 sts, hdc in next 5 sts, work st pat 1 over next 12 sts; rep from * once, sl st in first st to join.

Follow cable patterns above until you've worked two full repeats of st pat 3; then work five rounds of hdc to form top edge of bag. Fasten off, and weave in loose ends.

FINISHING

See "Felting Basics" on pages 160 to 169. The bag is hard-felted. Check and measure your bag frequently during the felting process. Felt and block the bag to the finished-size measurements. Lay the bag flat to dry.

LINING THE BAG

Trace the bottom of the bag onto the sheet of plastic canvas, and cut it out along the marked lines. Use the plastic canvas as a pattern to cut out the lining fabric for the bottom of the bag, adding 2" (5.1cm) to all sides. Set the plastic and the lining pieces aside.

Use the bag as a pattern to cut out the lining fabric for the interior of the bag. Wrap the lining fabric around the bag, aligning the top edge of the fabric to the top edge of the bag, overlapping the excess fabric and using straight pins to secure it. Trim off the excess fabric at the overlap and the bottom of the bag, leaving 2" (5.1cm) for seams. With right sides together, sew the short sides of the lining fabric together. Sew on the bottom-lining piece.

Glue the piece of plastic to the bag's bottom. Insert the lining into the bag. Fold the top edge of the lining to the wrong side, and tack it in place using glue.

Center and glue the handles to the inside front and back of the bag as shown. Use a tapestry needle and yarn to whipstitch the handles in place. Sew the top edge of the linining to the bag.

Jambières

Leg warmers are traditionally a dancer's accessory, but the fashion world adopted them, making them a trendy "must-have" for everyone. Our "Jambières" are worked in Tunisian crochet, which creates a softer fabric with more drape than standard crochet stitches. The resulting leg warmers are soft and scrunchy, not stiff—even after felting.

Before Felting

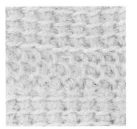

After Felting

skill level

Intermediate

finished size*

(*completed legwarmers after felting and before assembling)

- **Small/Medium:** 12" (30.5cm) wide and 18" (45.7cm) long
- **Large/X-Large:** 14" (35.5cm) wide and 18" (45.7cm) long

before-felting (B/F) measurements

- **Small/Medium:** 13" (33.0cm) wide and 16" (40.6cm) long
- **Large/X-Large:** 15" (38.1cm) wide and 16" (40.6cm) long

materials

- Brown Sheep Yarn Company Nature Spun Sport: 100% wool (184 yds. (168.2m) / 1¾ oz. (50 g)), color #N91 Aran, 3 skeins

notions

- Tapestry needle

hooks

- J/10 (6.00mm), or size needed to obtain gauge
- 10" (25.4cm) Tunisian/Afghan hook, or size needed to obtain gauge

gauge

- 16 sts and 13 rows of Stitch Pattern = 4 in. (10.2cm) square before felting
- 16 sts of Stitch Pattern = 3¾ in. (9.5cm) and 13 rows of stitch pattern = 4½" (11.4cm) after felting

notes

- Tunisian Crochet, or Afghan stitch, is worked with long hooks available in the same range of thicknesses as traditional crochet hooks. Tunisian crochet hooks are longer than standard crochet hooks; they hold loops created on first (Forward) half of row before working them off on Return row.
- Each row is worked in two parts: first or "Forward" row is worked from right to left by pulling up loops onto hook. On second (or Return row), these loops are worked off again as hook travels back from left to right.

- Afghan crochet is nearly always made without turning. Therefore, right side is always facing you.

- Pattern is worked from side to side.

abbreviations

See page 141.

special abbreviations

Tss: Tunisian simple stitch
Tps: Tunisian purl stitch

Jambières

STITCH PATTERN
Row 1: Work as basic Forward and Return row.
Row 2: With 1 loop on hook, * work 5 Tss into each of next 5 sts, work 3 Tps into each of next 3 sts, rep from * to end. Work plain Return row.
Rep Row 2 for pattern.

FORWARD ROW
(Worked only on first row)
Working into loop of each chain, insert hook into second chain from hook, yo, pull up a loop and leave on hook.
Insert hook into next chain, yo, pull up a loop and leave on hook; rep in each chain to end, or until required number of loops are on hook. Do not turn.

RETURN ROW
Yo, draw through one loop (this chain forms the edge stitch).
Yo, and draw through two loops.
Rep step 2 until one loop remains on hook. Do not turn. Loop remaining on hook becomes first stitch of following row.

TUNISIAN SIMPLE STITCH (Tss)
Insert hook from right to left behind single vertical thread.
Yo, draw loop through, and leave on hook.
Rep for required number of sts; then work Return row.

TUNISIAN PURL STITCH (Tps)
Bring yarn to front. Insert hook as for Tunisian Simple Stitch.
Take yarn to back of work and yo. Draw loop through, and leave on hook.
Rep for all sts as required, then work Return row.

LEG WARMERS
(Make 2.)
Chain 52 (60).
Pick up loop in second chain from hook, and following Stitch Pat, work until piece measures 16" (40.6cm) from foundation row.
Fasten off, leaving 30" (76.2cm) tail.

FINISHING
Using tail of yarn, sew long side edges together.
Weave in ends.

FELTING
Note: the Tunisian crochet stitch, when felted, will elongate slightly.
The leg warmers are soft-felted. See "Felting Basics" on pages 160 to 169. Check and measure your leg warmers frequently during the felting process. Felt and block them to the finished-size measurements. Lay them flat to dry.

STYLE TIP
Leg warmers are no longer considered practical accessories to be worn in cold weather only. They have become an all-season essential that can pull an outfit together. For downtown style, wear leg warmers with boots and a mid-calf peasant skirt (let a few lacy slips show at the hem). For an uptown look, wear them with ballet flats and a vintage skirt in satin.

Coordinate the "Jambières" leg warmers with the luxurious "Lacewing" scarf on page 100. The combination of accessories can be worn with an outfit that is an eclectic mix of dressy and casual pieces. Here, a cotton~ weave dress in a soft sage green is accented by a wide belt with metallic detailing~ its silver patina is echoed in the sexy spike heels. The surprising mix of separates has unique style.

Chocolate Velvet

You can turn simple shapes into great-looking garments by giving them a little twist. Here, a basic wrap becomes a shoulder-hugging capelet when the ends of one side of the crocheted fabric are threaded through a "keyhole" in the other side of the piece and sewn together. The resulting Twist detail adds soft folds to the front of the capelet. Made in a lofty, single-ply yarn that feels wonderful in your hands, the yarn develops a velvety fuzz when it is felted, adding interesting textural appeal.

skill level

Intermediate

finished size*

(*completed capelet after felting and before assembling)

- **Small/Medium:** 52" (132.1cm) long and 12" (30.5cm) long before assembling
- **Large/X-Large:** 58" (147.3cm) bust and 15" (38.1cm) long

before-felting (B/F) measurements

- **Small/Medium:** 58" (147.3cm) long and 20" (50.8cm) wide before assembling
- **Large/X-Large:** 68" (172.7cm) long and 24" (61.0cm) wide before assembling

materials

- MC: Malabrigo Merino Worsted; 100% Merino (216 yds. (197.5m) / 3½ oz. (100g)), color Rich Chocolate, 5 skeins
- CC (for optional edging): Lion Brand Fun Fur; 100% polyester (57 yds. (52.1m) / 1½ oz. (40g)), color 320-134 Copper, 2 skeins

notions

- Tapestry needle

hooks

- J/10 (6.00mm), or size needed to obtain gauge
- G/6 (4.25mm) for edging

gauge

- 10 sts and 8 rows of Stitch Pattern = 4" (10.2cm) square before felting
- 10 sts of Stitch Pattern = 2½" (6.4cm) and 8 rows of Stitch Pattern = 3½" (8.9cm) after felting

notes

- Turning chain does not count as stitch unless otherwise noted.

abbreviations

See page 141.

Before Felting

After Felting

Chocolate Velvet

SPECIAL ABBREVIATIONS
Hdc2tog: (Yo, insert hook in next st, yo and draw up a loop) twice, yo and draw through all 5 loops on hook.

STITCH PATTERN
Row 1: Ch 2, hdc across, turn.
Row 2: Ch 2, hdc across, turn.
Row 3: Ch 3, dc in 1st hdc and each hdc across, turn.
Rep. Rows 1–3 for pattern.

CAPELET
Using MC and larger hook, ch 51 (61).
Row 1: Hdc in 2nd ch from hook and in each st across (50 (60) hdc).

HELPFUL TIP

The secret to creating the twist detail in the capelet is its keyhole construction: two short fabric bands extend from each end of the crocheted fabric. One set is sewn together to make a keyhole; one end of the second set is threaded through the keyhole and joined to the opposite end.

Beginning with Row 2, follow Stitch Pattern, repeating Rows 1–3 until work measures 39 (49)" (99.1 (124.5) cm), ending with Row 1.

SHAPE RIGHT FRONT BANDS
The twisted loop portions at the front of the capelet are worked in two pieces, one at a time.

FIRST RIGHT FRONT BAND
Row 1: Ch 2, hdc across first 25 (30) sts, turn, leaving rem. sts unworked (25 (30) hdc).
Row 2: Ch 3, dc across, turn.
Row 3: Ch 2, hdc to last 2 sts, hdc2tog, turn (24 (29) hdc).
Row 4: Ch 2, hdc2tog, hdc across, turn, (23 (28) hdc).
Row 5: Ch 3, dc to last 2 sts, dc2tog, turn, (22 (27) hdc).
Row 6: Ch 2, hdc2tog, hdc across, turn, (21 (26)) hdc).
Row 7: Ch 2, hdc to last 2 sts, hdc2tog, turn, (20 (25) hdc).

Work even in rows of hdc until piece measures 9½" (24.1cm) from beginning of shaping.
Fasten off.

SECOND RIGHT FRONT BAND
Using sl st, attach yarn to outside edge of last full row before beg of First Right Front Band. Work as for First Right Front Band.

SHAPE LEFT FRONT BANDS
Using sl st, join yarn to outside edge of foundation ch and work as for Right Front Bands.

FINISHING
Weave in ends.

FELTING
See "Felting Basics" on pages 160 to169. Check and measure your capelet frequently during the felting process. Felt and block to finished-size measurements, and lay the capelet flat to dry.

ASSEMBLING
RIGHT FRONT
With right sides together, match up top edges of each Right Front Band. Sew these edges together to create the keyhole opening.

CREATE TWIST
Thread the bottom piece of the Left Front through the keyhole just made. Sew it to the corresponding top piece as for Right Front.

(OPTIONAL) EDGING
Using two strands of CC and smaller hook, join yarn to bottom edge of capelet. Sc evenly around bottom edge. Join with sl st. Ch 1, sc in each st around, sl st to join. Fasten off. Weave in remaining ends.

The smooth lines and delicate detail of "Chocolate Velvet" combine for an instant "put together" look. Slip into the capelet before a last~minute office meeting for a boost of confidence, or add it to your weekend wardrobe for Saturday~night style.

Crochet and Felting Basics

Tools • Materials • Techniques

This section is designed to be a helpful
at-your-fingertips reference guide
to the basics of felted crochet
as they apply to the beautful designs in
"the collection."

Getting Started

If you're new to crochet, you'll find all of the information that you'll need in this section—from the essential tools and techniques for traditional crochet to the more intricate procedures needed to crochet a variety of textured stitches. If you already crochet but you're new to felting, be sure to read "Felting Basics" on pages 160 to 169. All the essential tools and techniques for felting by hand and felting by machine are explained and illustrated for easy reference. There are also troubleshooting tips so that you can felt with confidence. Felting is an inexact, but inspiring, craft when combined with crochet. Have fun!

basic tools

Although a hook and yarn are all that you need to crochet, there are a few extra tools to add to your workbasket that will make your projects easier and more fun. There is an endless variety of hooks and tools. Here are some of my favorites:

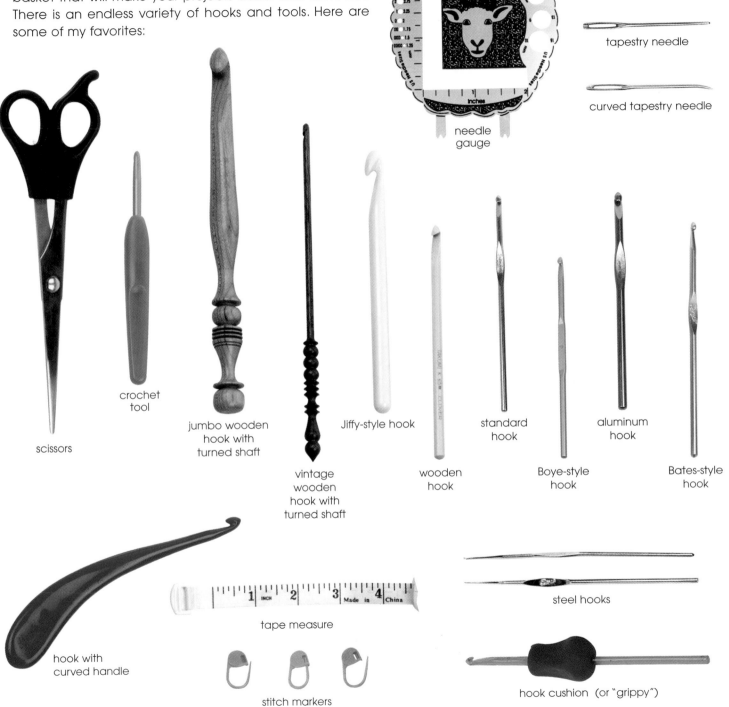

needle gauge

tapestry needle

curved tapestry needle

scissors

crochet tool

jumbo wooden hook with turned shaft

vintage wooden hook with turned shaft

Jiffy-style hook

wooden hook

standard hook

Boye-style hook

aluminum hook

Bates-style hook

hook with curved handle

tape measure

stitch markers

steel hooks

hook cushion (or "grippy")

hooks

Crochet hooks come in a variety of shapes, sizes, and materials, and you'll soon develop personal preferences depending on the yarns you use and the items you like to make. Some crocheters prefer Boye-style hooks; some prefer Bates. Some prefer metal to bamboo or plastic to wood, and vice versa. What matters is what you like and what works best for you. Experiment with different hook types as you try new patterns or yarns. You will find that different yarns will behave differently on hooks made of different materials—100 percent wool yarn behaves differently than wool blends on bamboo; metal hooks are more slippery, especially when crocheting with cotton yarns. Switch hooks if you are having any trouble working with a particular yarn.

b.

a.

finding the right hook

If a crochet pattern calls for a specific hook size, it's always a good idea to use that hook to make a gauge swatch before beginning the project. Gauges vary from one crocheter to the next. The gauge that is listed in each of the patterns is specifically designed for felting so that you might feel as though you're working your stitches a bit loosely for a conventional crochet project. Looser crochet is desirable because it provides room for the stitches to felt. Be sure to follow the instructions in order to create a crochet fabric that does not deviate too far from the pattern's requirements.

CROCHET HOOKS

US	METRIC
B/1	2.25mm
C/2	2.75mm
D/3	3.25mm
E/4	3.50mm
F/5	3.75mm
G/6	4.00mm
G	4.25mm
7	4.50mm
H/8	5.00mm
I/9	5.50mm
J/10	6.00mm
K/10½	6.50mm
L/11	8.00mm
M/N-13	9.00mm
N/P-15	10.00mm
P/Q	15.00mm
Q	16.00mm
S	19.00mm

ANATOMY OF A HOOK

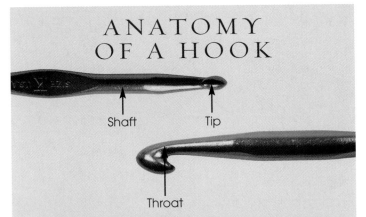

Shaft   Tip

Throat

Crochet hooks are composed of three sections: the tip, the throat, and the shaft. Boye and Bates hooks have different throat shapes, which can affect the way they interact with different yarns. A tapered throat is often easier to use when working with finer yarns. Pictured opposite are the Boye-style hook (a.) and the Bates-style hook (b.). Both have tapered throats.

Note: you may find that grasping a metal hook, or any other crochet hook, over a long period of time can aggravate carpal-tunnel syndrome or other wrist problems. To remedy this, try using a hook cushion, which is slipped around the hook's shaft like a snug, padded muff. It can make a big difference in your comfort level. Or take breaks, laying your work aside to ease any wrist tension.

TIP
When choosing your crochet hook, first refer to the size of the hook by its metric measurement because the letter used to identify the hook may not be standard from one manufacturer to another.

HOOKS BY PROJECT

PROJECT	SIZE	MM
Allotrope	H/8	5.00
	E/4	3.50
Amaranth	K/10½*	6.50
	J/10	6.00
	11**	8.00
Andean Button Scarf	K/10½	6.50
Andean Mittens	K/10 ½	6.50
Aran	H/8	5.00
Blue Flower	K/10½	6.50
Chocolate Velvet	J/10	6.00
	G/6	4.00
Clematis	G/6	4.00
	K/10½	6.50
Coral Reef	H/8	5.00
	G/6	4.00
Delicata	I/9	5.50
Fairy Floss	I/9	5.50
	G/6	4.00
Fedora	I/9	5.50
Jambières	J/10*	6.00
Lacewing	N/13	9.00
Lattice	H/8	5.00
Peony	H/8	5.00
	J/10	6.00
Picot Fan	H/8	5.00
	G/6	4.00
Rock Creek	J/10	6.00
Sand and Sea	I/9	5.50
	J/10*	6.00
Siberian Jewel	M/13	9.00
Snowberry	H/8	5.00
Spanish Moss	J/10	6.00
Tartan	G/6	4.00
Victoria	H/8	5.00
Wine and Roses	G/6	4.00
	F/5	3.75

Note: (*) indicates afghan needle
(**) indicates knitting needles

gauge

Gauge is a measurement of the number of stitches and the number of rows needed to make 1 inch (or centimeter) of crocheted fabric. When it comes to crocheting garments and accessories, especially those that are going to be felted, correct gauge is probably the single most important factor in making garments that fit and are comfortable to wear. Get into the habit of making gauge swatches for all of the items that you crochet. If you own a needle/hook gauge, such as the one pictured on page 133, you already have a simple way to check the size of your swatch. But if not, all you need is a ruler or measuring tape and a little patience. Place the measuring device on top of a square swatch crocheted with the yarn and the hook that you plan to use. The swatch should be at least 4 inches (10.2cm) square if you are doing traditional crochet only, but for felted crochet, the swatch should be a 10-inch (25.4cm) square. To calibrate the gauge, count the number of stitches and rows, and make a note of them. Count the stitches from left to right and the rows from top to bottom. Compare the numbers with those noted in the pattern—if you have more stitches than you should, switch to a bigger hook, and make another swatch. If you have fewer stitches, switch to a smaller hook. Even fractions of a stitch can add up to a big difference in a finished garment, so pay attention to these increments as well. Note that the gauges given in the patterns assume that the projects are going to be felted.

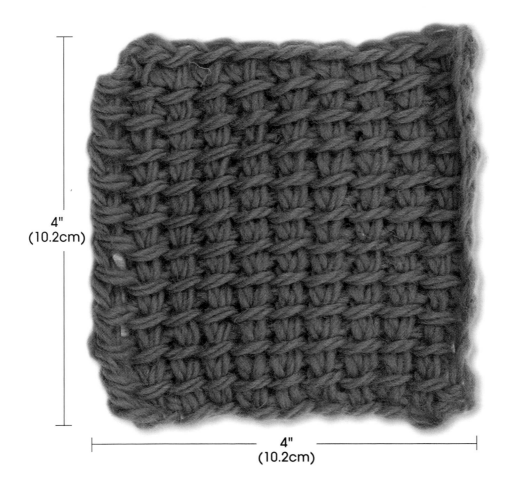

4"
(10.2cm)

4"
(10.2cm)

We crocheters take great delight in the visual and tactile aspects of the craft. As you stitch, you feel the yarn between your fingers and watch the colors change, stitch by stitch. In *The Color Book of Felted Crochet*, there is a dual creative focus—color and felting. You will notice that all the featured yarns contain at least 50 percent animal fibers, which take dye differently from those made from synthetic or plant fibers. The colors appear richer and slightly variegated—a red color might be brighter in a yarn made from alpaca than one made from wool. There's a wonderful range of natural-looking colors, such as rich brown, earthy cream, and subtle charcoal and gray, in yarns spun from

sheep, alpaca, and rabbit. These subtle colorways add depth and texture to the crocheted fabric. While each project in this book is crocheted in a particular color, feel free to select your own. If you decide to substitute a yarn, try to match the fiber content to the recommended yarn. Then make a swatch, and felt it to find out whether the new yarn is right for the project.

Our second focus is felting. When any crocheted fabric made from animal fiber is treated to heat, moisture, and friction, it goes through changes that transform the fabric from one that drapes and has visible stitches to one that has less drape and little to no stitch definition; it is also thicker and more solid in

YARNS BY PROJECT

PROJECT	YARN COMPANY	YARN NAME	COLOR & NUMBER
Allotrope	Brown Sheep Company	Nature Spun Sport	Charcoal #99
Amaranth	Cascade Yarns	Eco+	Fuschia #6913
	Gedifre	Gigante	#2358
Andean Button Scarf	Blue Sky Alpacas	Sport Weight	Natural White #500
Andean Mittens	Blue Sky Alpacas	Sport Weight	Natural White #500
Aran	Patons	Classic Merino Wool	Natural Mix #00229
Blue Flower	Blue Sky Alpacas	Melange	Cornflower #800
Chocolate Velvet	Malabrigo	Merino Worsted	Rich Chocolate
	Lion Brand	Fun Fur	Copper #320-134
Clematis	Berrocco	Ultra Alpaca	#6280
	Blue Sky Alpacas	Sport Weigh/Melange	#500,800
Coral Reef	Classic Elite Yarns	Lush	Coral #4480
Delicata	Cascade Yarns	220 Heathers	#2437
Fairy Floss	Cascade Yarns	Indulgence	#528
Fedora	Vermont Organics	O-Wool Classic	Cornflower
Jambières	Brown Sheep Company	Nature Spun Sport	Aran #N91

appearance. The bounce, softness, drape, and stretch of yarn made from animal fibers are different from yarns made from synthetics and plant fibers (which do not felt).

In addition to our focus on color and felting, we feature yarns that have a background story. For example, the "Rock Creek" vest on page 112 is made with *Be Sweet* mohair that is dyed and spun by a co-op of women in a job-creation program in South Africa. The "Lattice" bag on page 104 is worked in *Vermont Organics O-Wool Classic*, which comes from Merino sheep raised organically on farms in the United States; the yarn is dyed and spun in Vermont

according to strict environmental standards.

Of course, part of what makes any project your own is the choice of yarn, so we've tried to make it as easy as possible for you to select yarns that are readily available, that are suited to the style of the project, and that produce good felting results. When you choose a yarn, always read the label before you buy it. Also remember to make a test swatch to obtain the required gauge. Then felt your swatch to make sure that you understand how to get good felting results. Keep track of your felting trials using the tables on pages 170–171. In this way, you will be able to figure out what combination of variables works best.

YARNS BY PROJECT (CONT'D.)

PROJECT	YARN COMPANY	YARN NAME	COLOR & NUMBER
Lacewing	Blue Sky Alpacas	Brushed Suri	#900
Lattice	Vermont Organics	O-Wool Classic	Saffron
Peony	Patons Yarns	Classic Merino Wool	Black #0026; Aran #0202; Leaf Green #0240
Picot Fan	Classic Elite Yarns	Lush	Aqua Foam #4420
Rock Creek	Be Sweet	Bouclé Mohair	Slate
Sand and Sea	Cascade Yarns	Quatro	#9434
	Cascade Yarns	Fixation	Taupe #7360
Siberian Jewel	Be Sweet	Bouclé Mohair	Pale Amethyst
Spanish Moss	Cascade Yarns	Di.ve' Autunno	#32965
Snowberry	Patons Yarns	Classic Merino Wool	Rosewood #77414
Tartan	Patons Yarns	Classic Merino Wool	Black #00226; Aran #00202; Leaf #00240; Forest #77014
Victoria	Patons Yarns	Classic Merino Wool	Black #0026
Wine and Roses	Brown Sheep Company	Nature Spun Sport	Scarlet #N48S

Crochet Techniques

Simply put, crochet is about the simple loop. Made singly or in an intricate series, crocheted loops combine to resemble exquisitely textured fabrics depending on the hook used, the yarn chosen, and the stitch combinations worked. All of the essentials of crochet are included in this section, a veritable minicourse in the art of crochet. If you are just beginning to learn and a crochet hook is unfamiliar to you, take a bit of time to practice the basic stitches. To begin, choose a plain, smooth yarn because it is easier to see the stitches as they are made. Once your hands get used to the manipulations and you learn the basic stitches, you will be able to increase the number and intricasies of the stitches you make. All of the stitches are explained and illustrated in step-by-step photographs so that you can follow them while making loop after loop until you have developed confidence (and practical swatches that can be turned into a pretty blanket). Soon crochet will become second nature to you, and you will be inspired to crochet one of the great-looking projects in "The Collection." Simply use your imagination, and have fun!

General abbreviations are listed in the box on the opposite page. You'll find pattern-specific stitches defined within each project.

ABBREVIATIONS

( )	work the instructions within parentheses as many times as directed
* *	repeat the instructions between asterisks as many times as directed, or repeat from a given set of instructions
*	repeat the instructions following the single asterisk as directed
( )	work the instructions within brackets as many times as directed
"	inch(es)
alt	alternate
approx	approximately
beg	begin/beginning
bet	between
BL	back loop(s)
bo	bobble
BP	back post
BPdc	back post double crochet
BPsc	back post single crochet
BPtr	back post treble crochet
CA	color A
CB	color B
CC	contrasting color
ch	chain stitch
ch-	refers to chain or space previously made: e.g., ch-1 space
ch-sp	chain space
CL	cluster
cm	centimeter(s)
cont	continue
dc	double crochet
dc2tog	double crochet 2 stitches together
dec	decrease / decreases / decreasing
dtr	double treble
FL	front loop(s)
foll	follow / follows / following
FP	front post

FPdc	front post double crochet
FPsc	front post single crochet
FPtr	front post treble crochet
g	gram
hdc	half double crochet
inc	increase / increases / increasing
lp(s)	loops
m	meter(s)
MC	main color
mm	millimeter(s)
oz	ounce(s)
p	picot
pat(s) or patt	pattern(s)
pc	popcorn
pm	place marker
prev	previous
rem	remain/remaining
rep	repeat(s)
rnd(s)	round(s)
RS	right side
sc	single crochet (a.k.a. plain stitch)
sc2tog	single crochet 2 stitches together
sk	skip
Sl st	slip stitch
sp(s)	space(s)
st(s)	stitch(es)
tbl	through back loop
tch or t-ch	turning chain
tog	together
tr	treble crochet (a.k.a. triple)
trtr	triple treble crochet
WS	wrong side
yd(s)	yard(s)
yo	yarn over
yoh	yarn over hook

HOLDING THE HOOK

Learning to hold the crochet hook properly is the most important step in the process. Each crocheter generally has several different preferred methods for holding her hook and tensioning her yarn. Switching your tensioning method and the way you hold your hook can prevent repetitive stress injuries and tiredness. Here, the yarn is tensioned using the middle fingers of the yarn hand, and the hook is held in a "scoop" position. (You can also hold your hook as if it were a pencil if you prefer.)

MAKING A FOUNDATION CHAIN

Making a foundation chain is the first step in any crochet project. If you also knit, it's equivalent to casting on enough stitches for your first row of work. Unlike knitting, there are not multiple methods of creating a foundation chain. Be sure to keep your loops relatively loose so that they're easy to work into when you create your first row.

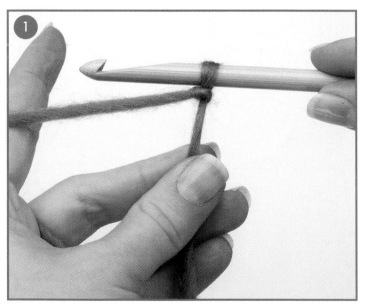

To begin foundation chain, make loose slipknot.
(See "Tip" on page 143.) Prepare for your first yarn over.

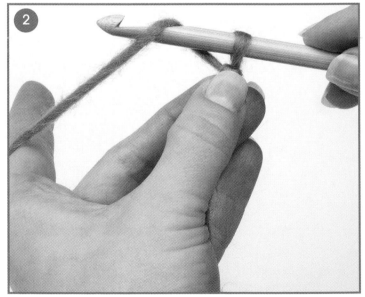

To make yarn over, dip hook to wrap yarn over hook and to maintain tension on yarn.

TIP

To make a slipknot, make a loop in the yarn about 6 in. (15.2cm) from the end. Insert the hook; catch the yarn; and pull a loop through. Pull softly on both ends to tighten the knot and to close the loop on the crochet hook.

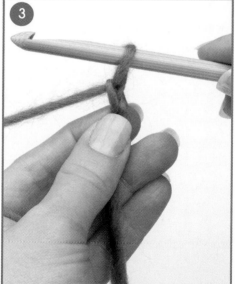

3

Pull yarn through slipknot. Note: you've just made the first link in the foundation chain.

4

Repeat steps 2–3, dipping hook, wrapping yarn, and pulling yarn through to make loops to create foundation chain. Note: the front side of the foundation chain resembles a braid.

5

The back side of the foundation chain has a line of "bumps" running down its center.

SLIP STITCH (SL ST)

Slip stitches are useful for many things, including joining together multiple pieces of crocheted fabric.

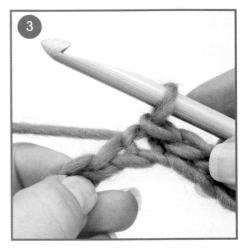

To begin slip stitch, insert hook into loop adjacent to loop on hook.

Dip hook, and wrap yarn over tip.

Draw yarn through loop to complete slip stitch. Continue to work across chain as desired.

SINGLE CROCHET (SC)

Now that you've learned how to make a foundation chain, you're ready to start crocheting. The first stitch that you will learn is called single crochet; it is one of the most common stitches, and it is often used for edgings. If you find patterns online, you may notice that the terminology is often different in the UK and elsewhere. Refer to the table on page 141 for both the US/UK stitch names and the international abbreviations that represent them.

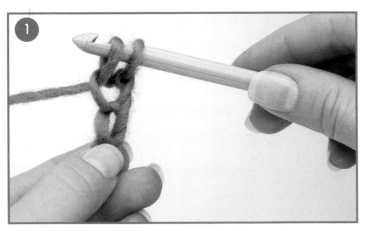

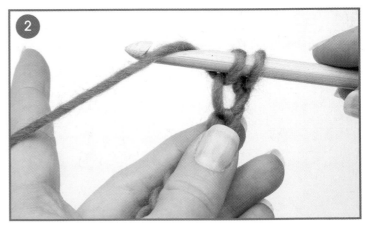

Insert hook from front to back into second stitch from hook. Dip hook, and wrap yarn over from back to front, drawing it through stitch to make two loops on hook.

Place yarn over hook from back to front. Rotate throat of hook toward you.

JOINING CHAINS INTO A ROUND

Chains are joined into a round to make some patterned stitches, such as flower shapes and granny squares.

Starting with foundation chain, insert hook into first chain stitch made. Dip tip of hook, and wrap yarn over hook from back to front.

Draw yarn through stitch and through loop on hook. Yarn over, completing joined chain in round.

Draw yarn through two loops on hook so that one loop remains, completing single crochet stitch.

HALF DOUBLE CROCHET (HDC)

Half double crochet is the next tallest stitch in crochet. It is formed similarly to single crochet but with extra loops for height.

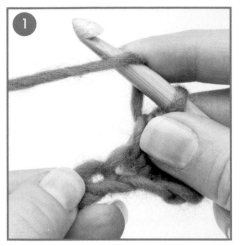

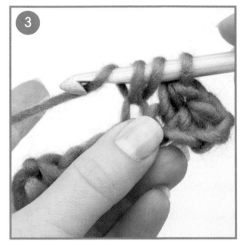

Starting with foundation chain, dip hook to wrap yarn over hook. Insert hook into third chain stitch from hook. Yarn over.

Pull wrapped hook through center of chain stitch, carrying wrapped yarn through stitch. Three loops remain on hook.

Yarn over. Draw yarn through all three loops on hook.

DOUBLE CROCHET (DC)

Double crochet is twice as tall as a single crochet stitch. It is a very common stitch in modern patterns.

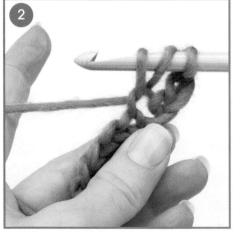

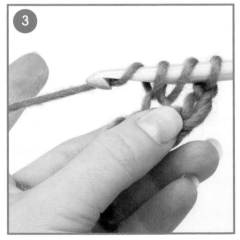

Starting with foundation chain, chain three stitches for turning chain. Yarn over hook from back to front.

Insert hook between two front loops and under back bump loop of fourth chain from hook.

Yarn over. Pull wrapped hook through center of chain stitch, and yarn over.

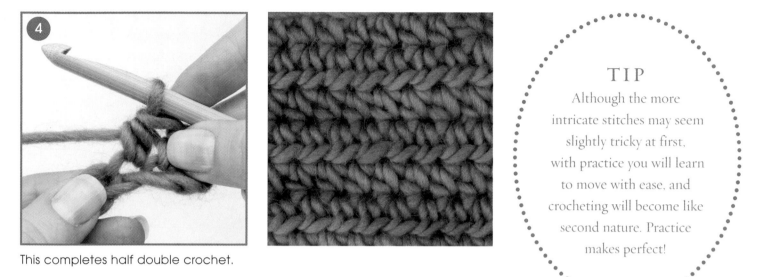

This completes half double crochet.

TIP
Although the more intricate stitches may seem slightly tricky at first, with practice you will learn to move with ease, and crocheting will become like second nature. Practice makes perfect!

Yarn over. Draw yarn through last two loops on hook.

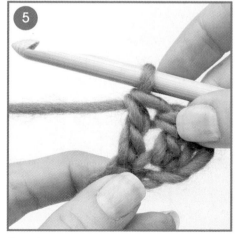

One loop remains on hook, completing double crochet stitch.

TREBLE CROCHET (TR)

Treble crochet, sometimes called "triple crochet," is the tallest, most commonly used crochet stitch.

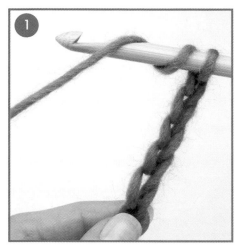

Starting from foundation chain, dip hook to wrap yarn over two times, moving from back to front.

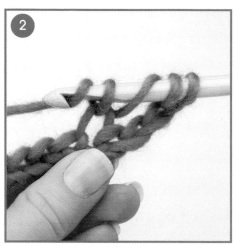

Insert hook into fifth loop in foundation chain. Dip hook to wrap yarn over from back to front. Four loops remain.

Draw yarn through first two loops.

Yarn over.

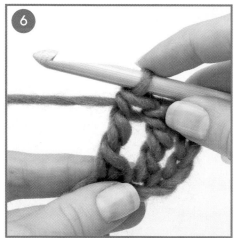

Draw through two loops, completing treble crochet.

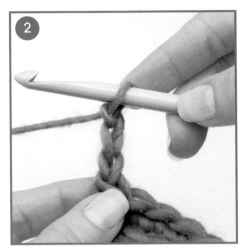

Yarn over, and draw through next two loops.

TURNING CHAINS

Turning chains are used to add height at the end of a row to continue stitching back across. They're made like a foundation chain and vary in length.

(sc) Start out by turning work to prepare for next row. Ch-1 stitch for turning chain. Insert hook front to back underneath top two loops of first stitch. Dip tip of hook to wrap yarn over hook. Draw yarn through stitch. Wrap yarn over hook. Draw yarn through two loops on hook. (One loop remains on hook.) This completes sc turning chain.

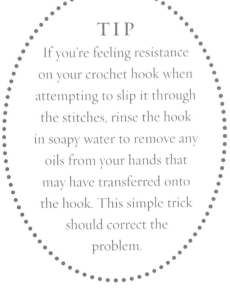

(dc) Start out by turning work so back side is facing you. Ch-3 stitches for turning chain. Dip tip of hook to yarn over hook. Skip first stitch of row directly below turning chain. Insert hook into next stitch down. Follow steps 2–5 in "Double Crochet," on pages 146 and 147, and continue to work one double crochet in top chain of previous row's chain. This completes dc turning chain.

TIP

If you're feeling resistance on your crochet hook when attempting to slip it through the stitches, rinse the hook in soapy water to remove any oils from your hands that may have transferred onto the hook. This simple trick should correct the problem.

WHICH LOOP?

One advantage that crochet has over knitting is the many different ways in which a stitch can be worked. There are different styles of knitting (American/English, Continental, or mixed) and different ways of holding or manipulating the yarn as it is worked, but in the end, the stitches look the same. In crochet, however, the way a

Back   Front

This is a view of a crochet stitch from above, showing the top two loops, one in front and one in back. Here, the hook is pointing to the space between the loops. The loop closer to you is the front loop. The loop farther away is the back loop.

Unless the pattern indicates otherwise, the hook is inserted through both loops when working any stitch.

AROUND THE POST, FRONT TO BACK

A post is the section between the top two loops and the base. To work "around the post, front to back," insert the hook around the **front** of the post of a stitch that is one or more rows below the row on which you are working.

On row of normal double crochet, turn, and make one dc stitch, yarn over, and insert hook from front to back between first and second double crochet on row below.

Yarn over, and draw yarn through loops on hook, completing front post double crochet.

stitch is worked—whether the hook is inserted into the front of the loop or the back, or if it is wrapped with yarn before being inserted—can have an effect on the appearance and texture of the stitch and the crocheted fabric. Even single crochet looks different when it is worked through the back loop only.

Stitches may be worked through the front loop only.

Stitches may be worked through the back loop only.

AROUND THE POST, BACK TO FRONT

If you are working "around the post, back to front," insert the hook around the **back** of the post of a stitch that is one or more rows below the row on which you are working. Stretch the fabric slightly to see the post, if necessary.

On row of normal double crochet, turn, and make one dc stitch, yarn over, and insert hook from back to front between first and second double crochet on row below.

Yarn over. Draw yarn through two loops on hook, completing back-post double crochet.

CROSSED STITCHES

You don't have to work stitches consecutively in crochet. It's simple to work them out of order or to skip stitches altogether to achieve particular effects. This crossed stitch is done in double crochet.

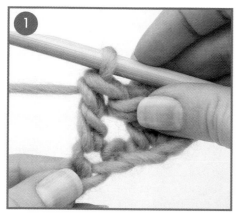

Skip stitch in row. Work one double crochet in next stitch.

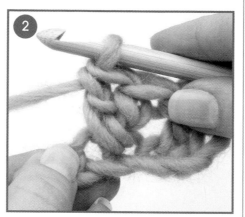

Working behind double crochet just made, work one double crochet in skipped stitch.

PUFF STITCH

Here, the stitch is worked into multiple times to create a cluster of half double crochet stitches.

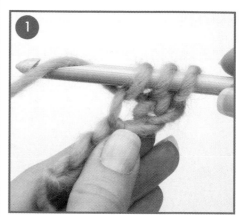

Starting with half double crochet stitch, dip hook to wrap yarn over from back to front, and insert hook into stitch. Yarn over. Draw yarn through stitch.

POPCORN STITCH

The popcorn stitch is created by working into a stitch multiple times. Performed at regular intervals, the popcorn shape can create an entire stitch pattern. Worked on a background of single crochet, the stitch is very visible.

Work five single crochet stitches into one stitch.

Remove hook from loop.

Insert hook from front to back under top two loops of first double crochet of group.

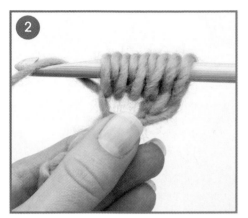

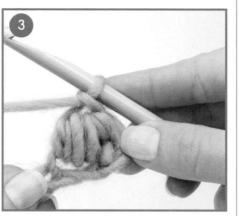

Here, the stitch is worked into multiple times to create a cluster of double crochet stitches.

Yarn over. Repeat step 1 two more times.

Yarn over. Draw yarn through loops on hook. Yarn over. Draw yarn through loop, leaving one loop on hook, completing puff stitch.

Work double crochet stitches, but insert hook in same stitch every time. Stitches held together at bottom will form shell shape.

Insert hook into dropped loop.

Draw yarn through stitch.

TIP
Such decorative stitches as the puff, shell, and popcorn are called relief stitches. They rise above the surface of the crocheted fabric, creating interesting texture and style in a finished piece.

INCREASING STITCHES (INC)

Shaping is essential to garment construction. It can make the difference between a garment that has a boxy, square shape to one that is formfitting yet comfortable. To make your crocheted pieces larger and smaller in certain places, such as the bodice or waist, you will need to increase and decrease the number of stitches worked. The pattern will indicate when you need to begin increasing or decreasing your stitches.

For single crochet stitch, work two single crochet stitches in one stitch at beginning, middle, or end of row, as directed in pattern.

Continue crocheting as directed in pattern, increasing as called for.

TIP

When increasing stitches, make sure to keep count of the stitches so that your numbers are always consistent in each project. You can increase at any point in a row.

DECREASING STITCHES (DEC)

Decreasing is when multiple stitches are drawn together into one. In steps 1–4, two single crochet stitches are worked together, and in steps A and B (page 155), two treble crochets are worked together.

For single crochet stitch, insert hook into next stitch. Dip hook to wrap yarn over from back to front. Draw yarn through stitch, making two loops on hook.

Insert needle into next stitch. Yarn over, drawing yarn through stitch only, making three loops on hook.

Yarn over.

Draw yarn through three loops on hook, leaving one loop on hook, completing decrease.

For treble crochet stitch, yarn over.

Draw yarn through three loops on hook, leaving one loop on hook, to complete decreasing treble crochet.

JOINING NEW YARN

There are two cases in which joining new yarn is necessary. In one case, you may wish to change the color of the yarn; in the second instance, you may have simply run out of yarn.

TIP

Different colors of yarn within the same brand can have varying textures due to the dye—darker dyes are often heavier. If your piece uses several yarn colors, test a swatch to see how it affects the rate of felting.

To join new yarn with double crochet, complete all but next-to-last stitch in row. Work last double crochet to point where only two loops are left on hook. Yarn over with old yarn and new yarn.

Draw new and old yarns through two loops on hook. Drop old yarn, and continue with new yarn.

Note: see "Fastening Off and Weaving in Ends," on opposite page.

JOINING TOGETHER/SEAMING

Sometimes you'll need to join two pieces of crochet together. The two most commonly used seaming methods are slip stitch and single crochet. Each has its advantages—the slip stitch is less bulky, and single crochet is sturdier. Making a bag? Use single crochet. A shoulder seam? Slip stitch may be the better choice.

Knitters: here's yet another reason to learn crochet. The slip stitch is a great way to seam cardigans or knitted pieces. If you are using a two- (or more) ply yarn and want to make your seam less bulky, pull apart the yarn and use only half of the plies for seaming.

To join together with single crochet, lay pieces right sides together. Match stitches across each side edge. Work through both pieces, and insert hook through top two loops of first two corresponding stitches. Yarn over. Pull yarn through both stitches on hook.

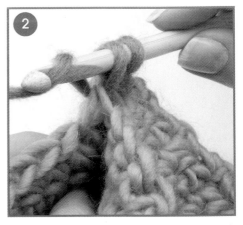

Insert hook through two front loops of next two corresponding stitches. Yarn over. Pull yarn through all loops.

FASTENING OFF AND WEAVING IN ENDS

Finishing a crochet project is simple. Because you're only working one stitch at a time, you have only one stitch to close at the end, after which the loose end is fastened off and anchored behind the stitches previously worked.

EDGING

For an edge in another color, use the slip stitch worked into the sides of the stitches and a second yarn.

Make last stitch so that only one loop remains on hook. Cut end of yarn about 6 in. (15.2cm) from end of hook.

Use hook to draw yarn's cut end through last loop on hook. Pull yarn tail to tighten. Thread end of yarn through tapestry needle, and weave tail up and down through several stitches. Repeat weaving in opposite direction to secure. Cut yarn.

Insert hook through double loops, and work evenly across edge, using decorative stitch of your choice. Consider adding an edge using double crochet stitches featured on page 146 or any other stitch that appeals to you.

Repeat step 2, continuing until pieces are joined together. Fasten off, and weave in ends, completing single crochet.

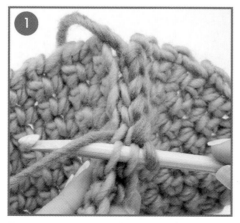

To join together with slip stitch, lay pieces together, matching stitches. Insert hook through back loops of first two corresponding stitches. Yarn over. Pull yarn through stitches.

Repeat step 1 in all corresponding stitches until pieces are joined together. Fasten off, and weave in ends, completing seaming with slip stitch.

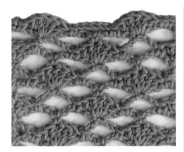

SHELL TRELLIS STITCH

Multiple of 12 sts + 1, (add 2 for foundation chain)

Row 1 (RS): Work 2 dc in 3rd ch from hook, *sk 2 ch, sc in next ch, ch 5, sk 5 ch, sc in next ch, sk 2 ch, 5 dc in next ch; rep from * to *, ending last rep with 3 dc in last ch, turn.

Row 2: Ch 1, sc in first st, *ch 5, sc into next ch-5 sp, ch 5, sc in 3rd dc of next 5-dc shell*, rep from * to *, ending last rep with sc in 3rd ch of beg ch-3, turn.

Row 3: Ch 5 (counts as dc, ch 2), sc into next ch-5 sp, 5 dc in next sc, sc into next ch-5 sp, *ch 5, sc into next ch-5 sp, 5 dc in next sc, sc into next ch-5 sp*, rep from * to *, ending ch 2, dc in last sc, turn.

Row 4: Ch 1, sc in first st, *ch 5, sc in 3rd dc of next 5-dc shell, ch 5, sc into next ch-5 sp*, rep from * to * across, ending last rep with sc in 3rd ch of beg ch-5, turn.

Row 5: Ch 3 (count as dc), 2 dc in first st, *sc in next ch-5 arch, ch 5, sc in next ch-5 arch, 5 dc in next sc *, rep from * to *, ending last rep with 3 dc in last sc, turn.

Rep Rows 2–5 for patt.

PEACOCK FAN STITCH

Multiple of 12 sts + 1, (add 1 for foundation chain)

Row 1 (RS): Sc in 2nd ch from hook, *sk 5 ch, 13 dtr in next ch, sk 5 ch, sc in next ch *, rep from * to * across, turn.

Row 2: Ch 5 (counts as dtr), dtr in first st, *4 ch, sk 6 dtr, sc in next dtr, 4 ch, sk 6 dtr, work (dtr, ch 1, dtr) all in next sc *, rep from * to *, ending last rep with sk 6 dtr, 2 dtr in last sc, turn.

Row 3: Ch 1, sc in first st, *sk (dtr and 4 ch), 13 dtr in next sc, sk (4 ch and dtr), sc in next ch-1 sp*, rep from * to * across, ending sc in 5th ch of beg ch-5, turn.

Rep Rows 2 and 3 for patt.

BASKET WEAVE STITCH

Rfdc–Round front double crochet: Yo, insert hook from the front around the post (or stem) of appropriate stitch, complete the double crochet.

Rbdc–Round back double crochet: Yo, insert hook from the back around the post (or stem) of appropriate stitch, complete the double crochet.

Multiple of 8 sts + 2, (add 2 for foundation ch)

Row 1 (WS): Sk 3 ch (counts as dc), dc in each ch across, turn.

Row 2–4: Ch 3 (counts as dc), *rfdc around each of next 4 sts, rbdc around each of next 4 sts *, rep from * to * across, dc in 3rd ch of beg ch-3, turn.

Row 5–7: Ch 3 (counts as dc), *rbdc around each of next 4 sts, rfdc around each of next 4 sts *, rep from * to * last st, dc in 3rd ch of beg ch-3, turn.

Rep Rows 2–7 for patt.

PICOT FAN STITCH

Multiple of 12 sts + 1, (add 1 for foundation chain)

Row 1 (RS): Sc in 2nd ch from hook, *ch 5, sk 3 ch, sc in next ch *, rep from * to * across, turn.

Row 2: Ch 5 (counts as dc, ch 2), *sc into next ch-5 arch, 8 dc into next ch-5 arch, sc into next ch-5 arch, ch 5 *, rep from * to * across, ending sc into last ch-5 arch, ch 2, dc in last st, turn.

Row 3: Ch 1, sc in first st, sk ch-2, sc in next sc, *(dc, picot) in each of first 7 dc of 8-dc group, dc in next dc, sc into next ch-5 arch *, rep from * to * across, ending sc in 3rd ch of beg ch-5, turn.

Row 4: Ch 8 (counts as dc, ch 5), sk 2 picot, *sc in next picot, ch 5, sk 1 picot, sc in next picot, ch 5, sk 2 picots, dc in next sc, ch 5, sk 2 picots *, rep from * to *, ending last rep with dc in last sc, turn.

Rep Rows 2–4 for patt.

POPCORN STITCH

Work 5 dc in same st, drop loop from hook, insert hook in first dc of 5-dc group, and pull dropped loop through loop on hook to close.

Multiple 4 sts + 1 (add 2 for foundation ch)

Row 1: Sk first 3 ch (counts as dc), dc in next ch and in each ch across, turn.

Row 2: Ch 3 (counts as dc), dc in next dc, popcorn in next dc, *dc in each of next 3 dc, popcorn in next dc*, rep from * to * across, ending dc in each of last 2 dc, working last dc in 3rd ch of beg ch-3, turn.

Row 3: Ch 3 (counts as dc), dc in each st across working last dc in 3rd ch of beg ch-3, turn.

Row 4: Ch 3 (counts as dc), dc in each of next 3 dc, *popcorn in next dc, dc in each of next 3 dc *, rep from * to * across, ending dc in 3rd ch of beg ch-3, turn.

Row 5: Rep Row 3.

Rep Rows 2–5 for patt.

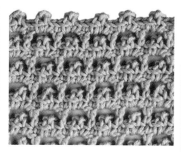

ARCH STITCH

Picot: ch 4, sl st in 4th ch from hook.

Multiple of 3 sts + 2

Row 1 (RS): Sc in 2nd ch from hook, sc in next ch, *picot, sc in each of next 3 sc*, rep from * to * across, ending sc in each of last 2 chs, turn.

Row 2: Ch 5 (counts as dc, ch 2), sk first 3 sc, dc in next sc, *ch 2, sk next 2 sc, dc in next sc *, rep from * to * across, turn.

Row 3: Ch 1, sc in first dc, *work (sc, picot, sc) all into next ch-2 sp, sc in next dc *, rep from * to * across, ending sc in 3rd ch of beg ch-5 of previous row, turn.

Rep Rows 2 and 3 for patt.

CROSS DOUBLE STITCH

Multiple of 2 sts (add 2 for foundation chain)

Special Abbreviation
2Cdc (2 cross double crochets): Sk next st, dc in next st, dc in skipped st working over previous dc.

Row 1 (RS): Sk 3 ch (count as dc), *work 2Cdc over next 2 chs *, rep from * to * across, ending dc in last ch, turn

Row 2: Ch 1, sc in each sc across, working last sc in 3rd ch of beg ch-3, turn.

Row 3: Ch 3 (counts as dc), sk 1st st, *work 2Cdc over next 2 sts *, rep from * to * across, ending dc in last st, turn.

Rep rows 2 and 3 for patt.

FAN STITCH

Multiple of 6 sts + 1, (add 1 for foundation ch)

Row 1 (RS): Sc in 2nd ch from hook, *sk 2 ch, 5 dc in next ch, sk 2 ch, sc in next ch*, rep from * to * across, turn.

Row 2: Ch 3 (counts as dc), 2 dc in first sc, *sc in 3rd dc of next 5-dc shell, 5 dc in next sc*, rep from * to * across, ending last rep with 3 dc in last sc, turn.

Row 3: Ch 1, sc in first dc, *5 dc in next sc, sc in 3rd dc of next 5-dc shell*, rep from * to * across, ending last rep with sc in 3rd ch of beg ch-3, turn.

Rep Rows 2 and 3 for patt.

Felting Basics

Have you ever accidentally put one of your wool sweaters in your washing machine's hot-wash cycle only to find it a size that would fit a baby when you pulled it out? If so, then you've already tried felting (or "fulling," which is the technical term for felting crocheted fabric). If at first your sweater had a visible stitch pattern, now you would notice that the pattern has a softer, less-defined look. In addition to shrinking, you might also notice that the fabric is thicker and has less drape. What has happened is that the wool has acted in a way that is natural to its properties—the microscopic scales that cover the outside of each animal hair (that is spun into stands to make yarn) have become entangled in adjacent scales, interlocking and forming a solid fabric. The felted (or fulled) fabric is warm and comfortable to wear and can be cut without fraying or raveling. After felting, you might also notice a "halo" over the surface of the crocheted fabric; this is fleece that has separated from the strands of yarn. Read "Felting By Machine," on page 166, to learn how to prevent clogging your machine (and the plumbing) when you felt.

In "Felting Basics," we'll walk you step-by-step through felting by hand and felting by machine—two different methods that produce felted fabric. We'll also include instructions for blocking and finishing your felted projects, as well as an invaluable troubleshooting guide to help you prevent or remedy problems that come up when you take part in this inexact, but thoroughly inspiring, craft.

CAUTION

It is important to follow the general recommendations for felting given in each set of directions. You will notice that two kinds of felting are featured: *soft-felting*, where the crocheted fabric goes through a short process that produces a fabric that retains some stitch definition and is slightly smaller than the original; and *hard-felting*, where the piece continues to be subjected to heat, moisture, and friction for a longer time until the fabric is thick and firm, and there is little or no stitch definition. In all cases, *soft-felt* or *hard-felt* to the measurements listed in the directions.

basic tools for crocheting (before felting)

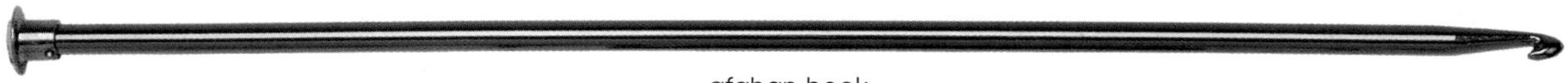

afghan hook

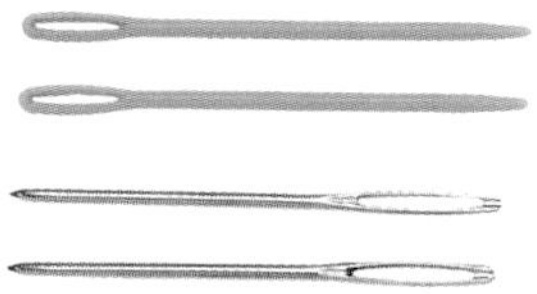

tapestry needles

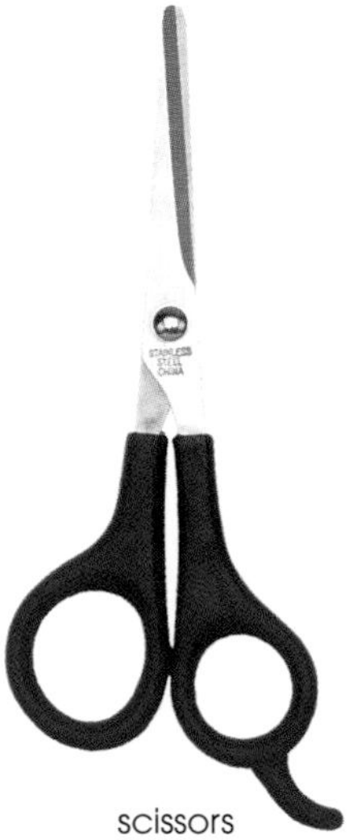

scissors

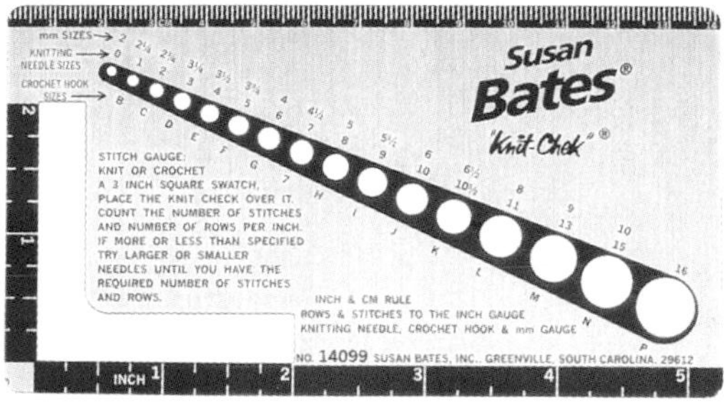
Susan Bates®
"Knit-Chek"®
STITCH GAUGE:
KNIT OR CROCHET
A 3 INCH SQUARE SWATCH,
PLACE THE KNIT CHECK OVER IT.
COUNT THE NUMBER OF STITCHES
AND NUMBER OF ROWS PER INCH.
IF MORE OR LESS THAN SPECIFIED
TRY LARGER OR SMALLER
NEEDLES UNTIL YOU HAVE THE
REQUIRED NUMBER OF STITCHES
AND ROWS.
INCH & CM RULE
ROWS & STITCHES TO THE INCH GAUGE
KNITTING NEEDLE, CROCHET HOOK & mm GAUGE
NO. 14099 SUSAN BATES, INC., GREENVILLE, SOUTH CAROLINA 29612

gauge for needles and crocheted fabric

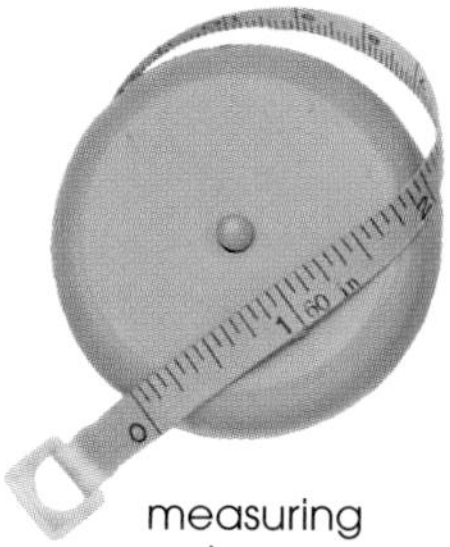

measuring tape

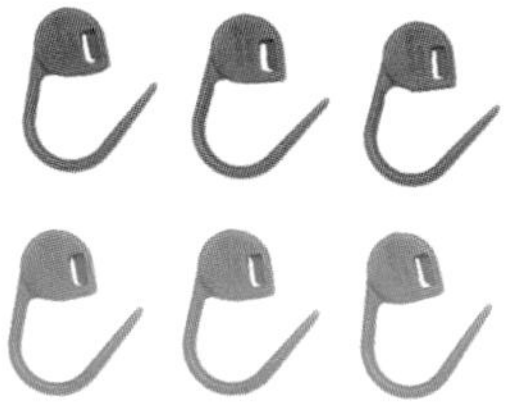

stitch markers

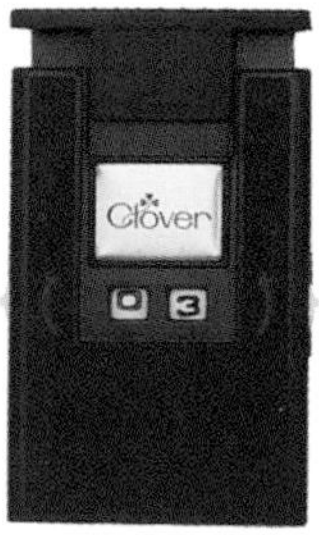
Clover

row counter

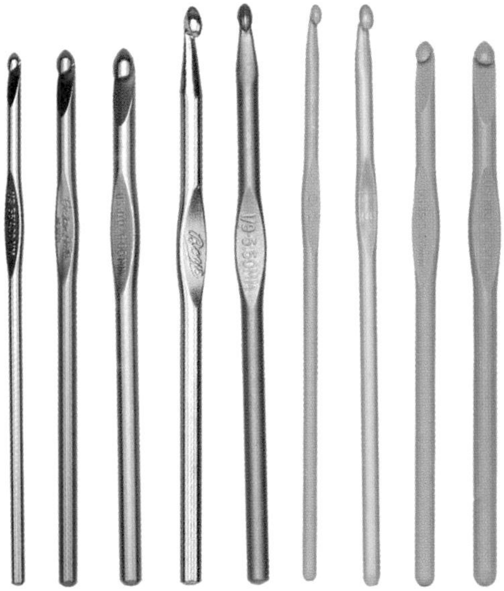

crochet hooks

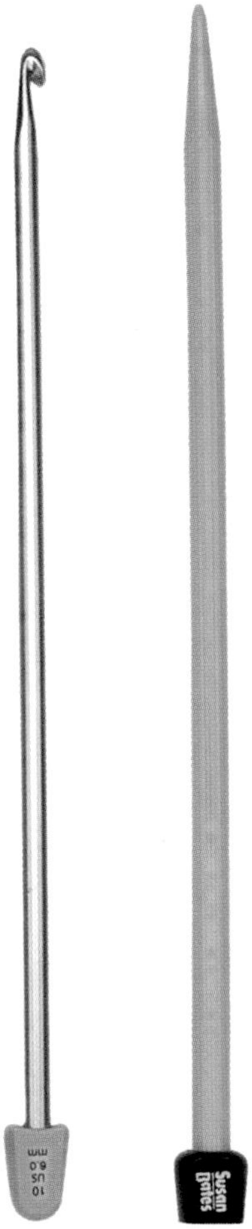
10 US 6.0 mm
Susan Bates

knitting needle

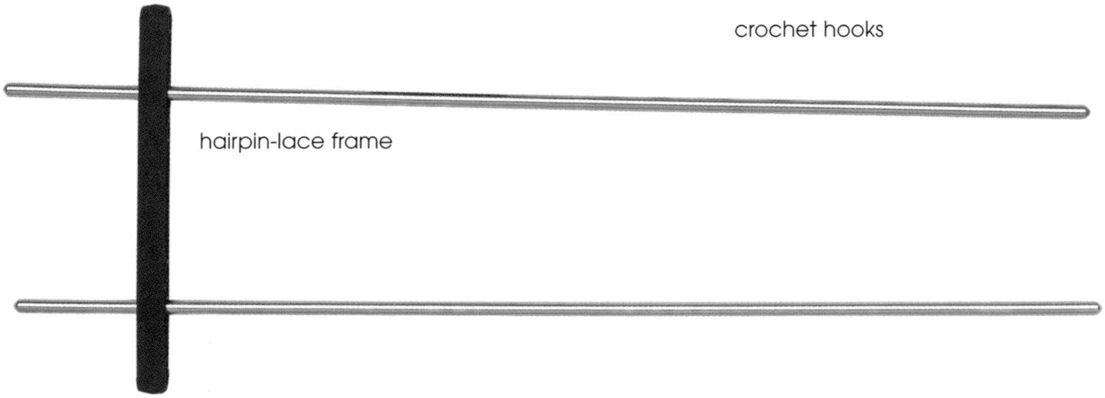

hairpin-lace frame

basic tools for felting

SUPPLIES FOR FELTING BY HAND

clean towel

clean dishpan (or tub)

mild detergent
(or shampoo)

timer

rubber gloves

OPTIONAL FELTING AIDS

nylon gloves

loofah mitts

SUPPLIES FOR FELTING BY MACHINE

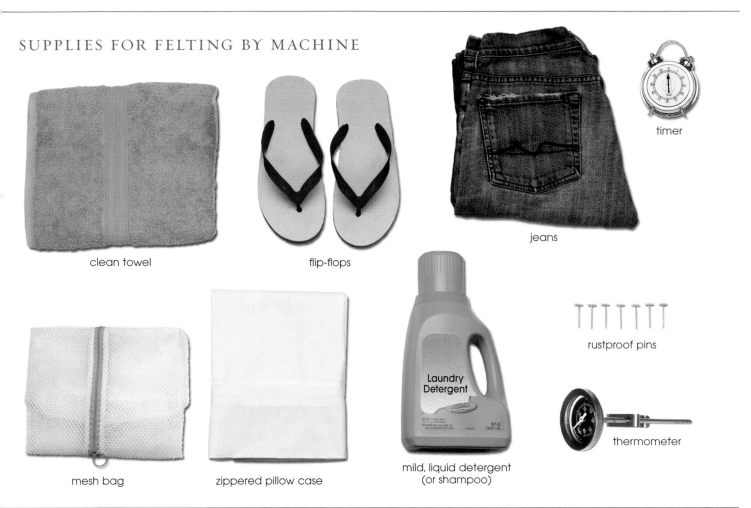

clean towel

flip-flops

jeans

timer

mesh bag

zippered pillow case

mild, liquid detergent
(or shampoo)

rustproof pins

thermometer

BLOCKING AIDS

bowls

FELTING BY HAND

Felting by hand is suitable for crocheted swatches and small projects, such as a scarf. To test the conditions that successfully felt crocheted fabric, crochet a 10-in.-square (25.4cm) swatch, using a hook in a size noted in the

Add enough hot water to a dishpan so that the crocheted swatch or item can be completely submerged. Add a small squirt of detergent to the water. Note the exact measurement of your swatch on the fill-in table.

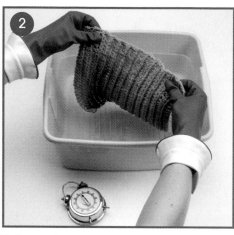

Put on rubber gloves, and use your hands to mix the water and liquid soap together. Set the timer for one minute; make a note of the time on the fill-in table. Submerge the swatch, and agitate it with your hands.

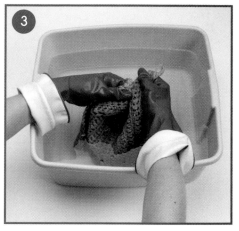

At one minute, check the swatch to see if the stitches have begun to blend together. If you wish to further the felted effect, continue to agitate the swatch. Reset the timer for another minute, and let the swatch soak. Then check the swatch, and make a note of the results.

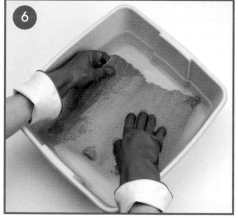

When the crocheted swatch has felted to the desired size, remove the swatch from the soapy water. Rinse the dishpan clean, and fill it with cool water. To stop the felting, rinse the felted swatch gently, without agitating it further.

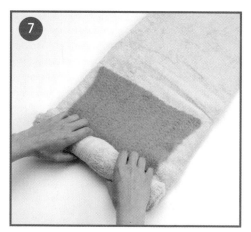

Gently squeeze out the excess water over the dishpan. Then lay the felted swatch on a towel, patting the felted fabric flat. Roll the swatch in the towel to remove any excess water.

Unroll the towel, and lay the swatch on a clean, dry towel. Use your hands and rustproof pins to shape and secure the felted swatch as shown. Allow the swatch to dry. (Thick, felted fabric may need to be flipped over and re-pinned so that both sides of the swatch dry.)

directions, or one necessary to obtain the gauge. Make a note of the soaking/agitation times on the tables provided on pages 170–171 so that you can replicate the same or similar effects in the corresponding project.

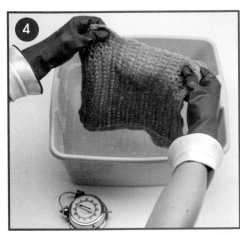

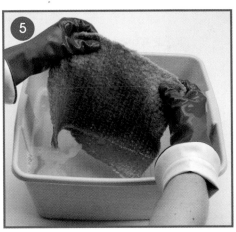

TIP
When agitating the fabric by hand, wear rubber gloves. If the water is still too hot, use a kitchen tool, such as a potato masher.

To *soft-felt* (where the stitches are still visible and the piece has shrunk only slightly), continue to step 6. To *hard-felt* (where the stitches are no longer visible, and the piece has shrunk to its maximum capacity), continue to step 5.

To hard-felt, keep agitating the swatch, allowing it to soak in the solution. Reset the timer for another minute. Continue as before, felting the fabric until the stitches are no longer visible, and the swatch has thickened.

SWATCH SAMPLES

Original 10-in. (25.4cm) swatch 100% wool US K10.5/6.50mm hook

Felting time: one minute

Felting time: two minutes

Felting time: seven minutes

felting techniques (cont'd.)

FELTING BY MACHINE

Felting by machine is a convenient and effective method of felting medium and large crocheted pieces, such as a shrug or a coat. One of the most important preparations for felting by machine is to protect the

Place the crocheted item in a mesh bag or a zippered pillowcase, zipping the bag or case closed.

On a top-loading washing machine, set the dials to "hot wash/cold rinse" and the longest cycle, ensuring that the tub fills with enough water to cover the garment. Add felting aids, such as flip flops or a pair of jeans, to help agitate smaller items. (Do not use towels or anything fuzzy to prevent adding lint to the soaking solution.)

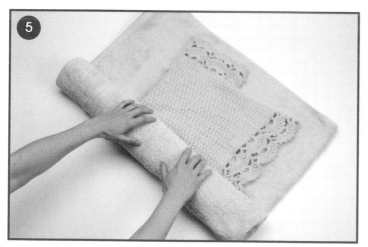

Once the piece is the required measurements and it has the desired felted effect, remove it from the tub, and rinse it in warm-to-cool (not cold) water without agitating it. Gently squeeze out the excess water using your hands. Lay the piece on a clean, dry towel, and roll it in the towel to remove more water.

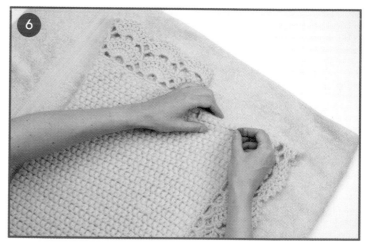

Block the felted piece on a dry towel, flattening and shaping the fabric with your hands. Use rustproof pins to secure the edges and all sections. For guidance, use the finished measurements listed in the pattern instructions and schematic drawings. Allow the piece to dry thoroughly.

machine from trapping any fiber in the process. For this, a mesh bag or zippered pillowcase is effective. Enclosing especially small items in a bag can prevent them from getting "lost" in the machine or in the plumbing.

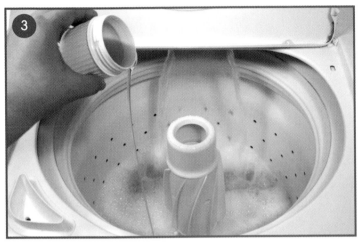

Add a very small amount of laundry detergent to the water in the tub. Put the filled bag into the tub, pushing it down to submerge it.

Set the timer to one minute. Then check the crocheted fabric to assess the felting, and make a note of the time. *To soft-felt*, agitate the item until the size of the piece is the same as the recommended measurements indicated in the project directions. *To hard-felt*, continue agitating the piece until the crochet stitches are no longer visible and the fabric is firm and thick.

helpful hints and tips for blocking and finishing

TECHNIQUES AND TOOLS

It is necessary to maintain the shape of a crocheted item that is felted until the fabric dries completely. To do this, use the following tools and techniques.

Hands
For flat items, you might simply need to "sculpt" the crochet fabric while it is wet or damp, using your fingers.

Rustproof Pins
After a flat piece of felted fabric is hand-shaped, reinforce the edges using rustproof pins placed strategically along the edges, especially those that curl up.

Molds
For dimensional pieces, use common household items, such as bowls and plastic containers, books covered in plastic, and crumpled-plastic bags to maintain the shape of your felted item until it dries.

When you're blocking bags and hats, or similar dimensional shapes, use any item that is the same shape and size as your project; a bowl is a good "mold" for a hat. The mold can be *slightly* larger than the project to retard any further shrinkage as the yarn dries. (If the project requires the tiniest bit of stretching to get it around the mold, that's fine.) Square and rectangular containers made of plastic work well for shaping tote bags, as do heavy books wrapped in plastic bags.

Plastic Bags
Stuffed loosely into sleeves or laid under collars, plastic bags can both support the shape of the item and allow air to circulate as the project dries. Simply crumple plastic bags, and stuff them loosely into the desired section to hold the drying layers apart. This method is especially helpful when drying long, cylindrically shaped items, such as leg warmers and coat sleeves. It is important *not* to stuff the sections tightly, which will keep air from circulating, slowing down the drying process.

HELPFUL TIPS

Sometimes, our felting projects don't turn out the way we expect. Unfortunately, you can't "un-felt" fabric, so the best cure is prevention.

* If you decide to substitute a yarn listed in the directions for another, try to match the fiber content of the new yarn to the recommended yarn. Make a swatch, and felt it to determine if the new yarn is right for your project.

* The best felting yarns are 100% wool or contain at least 50% animal fiber. Fiber blends, such as lamb's wool and nylon, also felt well. Merino, mohair, and cashmere felt well and have a soft hand, while Shetland wool felts well but feels scratchy on the skin.

* In general, many white, light-colored, and "superwash" yarns felt poorly or not at all because bleaching and chemical processes affect the "feltability" of the yarn.

* For machine-felting, open the top lid or pull out the power button of the machine to stop any agitation. While agitation advances the felting process, it can easily throw off your results, especially on larger, wearable items that need to fit.

* Loose crochet is ideal for felting because the tension between the stitches allows the strands of yarn to rub up against one another in the felting process. The more friction, the faster the yarn will felt.

* When felting by machine, set a timer at one-minute intervals for the first two minutes. Stop, and check your work often. Once the stitches begin to disappear, the rate of felting increases.

* A thermometer can provide an understanding of the role that temperature plays in felting—if the water is too cold, felting may not occur; if the water is too hot, the crocheted fabric may felt too quickly.

TROUBLESHOOTING

While it is important to try to control the rate of felting, the process is a fun and inexact art. You may find that unexpected scenarios occur.

❋ If your piece has not felted enough, continue the soaking/agitation process a little longer. If you are felting by machine, and you find that your item is *just* about the right size and texture, you might switch to agitating the piece by hand for more control.

❋ If you happen to overdo the felting—your crocheted item is a bit too small or misshapen—all is not lost. First, remember that blocking is your "friend." Use your hands to stretch the piece and/or sections *hard* while blocking it until it reaches the desired measurements.

❋ If the piece is still too small, add new, non-felted crocheted panels or extra strips to the felted garment so that the garment fits better. For example, you can create a narrow panel between the front and back sections of a sweater to make it fit. The contrasting textures of the felted and the non-felted sections can be very attractive.

❋ If a skirt, sleeve, or hem is too short, use one of the textured stitches featured on pages 158-159 to add a decorative edge and to make the piece longer.

❋ If the pieces are large enough but they are the wrong shape, alter them.
- If the piece is hard-felted, cut the fabric using scissors, either cutting off or trimming sections until you have the right shape and measurement.
- If the piece is soft-felted, use a fabric pencil to draw the actual pattern shape onto the fabric, and sew the project together along the marked lines.

Other Quick Fixes

❋ If your felted piece is too "hairy," use a dog brush to lift up the fibers. Gently stroke the surface of the felted fabric, lifting up the brush to raise the fibers. Use sharp scissors to trim off the fibers, being careful not to cut into the crocheted fabric.

❋ If you deem the item irretrievable, use the felted fabric to make other small projects, such as small purses, pot holders, and the like.

CARING FOR YOUR FELTED PIECES

For best results, dry clean them. You may also:
- wash them by hand, using a gentle soap and lukewarm water
- use a press cloth and a hot steam iron to press out creases and wrinkles, reshaping the piece while it is still warm and damp
- use a form to maintain the shape of your project when you are not wearing or using it
- Optional: put your project into a dryer set to "tumble dry" to fluff and dry it. Be aware that your piece may continue to felt, so it will still require careful watching. For such items as scarves or bags, a dryer presents minimal risk.

appendix: test-felting log

FELTING BY HAND

Use this table to keep track of details as you test-felt your swatches by hand. If desired, make a new copy of this table, adding columns for agitation time, kind of yarn (especially fiber content), type and amount of soap, and water temperature for a clear understanding of how different variables affect the felting results.

FELTING BY HAND				
PROJECT NAME	ORIGINAL SIZE	FELTING TIME	SIZE AFTER FELTING	NOTES

FELTING BY MACHINE

Use this table to keep track of details as you test-felt your swatches by machine. If desired, make a new copy of this table, adding columns for agitation time, kind of yarn (especially fiber content), type and amount of soap, and water temperature for a clear understanding of how different variables affect the felting results.

FELTING BY MACHINE				
PROJECT NAME	ORIGINAL SIZE	FELTING TIME	SIZE AFTER FELTING	NOTES

Sources and Resources

USA
YARNS

Berrocco
508-278-2527
www.berrocco.com

Be Sweet
415-331-9676
www.besweetproducts.com

Blue Sky Alpacas
888-460-8862
www.blueskyalpacas.com

Brown Sheep Company
800-826-9136
www.brownsheep.com

Cascade Yarns
www.cascadeyarns.com

Classic Elite Yarns
978-453-2837
www.classiceliteyarns.com

Gedifra
800-445-9276
www.westminsterfibers.com

Lion Brand
800-258-9276
www.lionbrand.com

Malabrigo
786-866-6187
www.malabrigoyarn.com

Patons
888-368-8401
www.patonsyarns.com

Vermont Organics (O-Wool)
802-388-1313
www.o-wool.com

NOTIONS AND TOOLS

Blue Moon Beads®
800-965-8746
www.bluemoonbeads.com

M&J Trimming
800-965-8746
www.mjtrim.com

Michaels Stores, Inc.
800-642-4235
www.michaels.com

P and S Fabrics
212-226-1534
www.psyarns.com

Tinsel Trading
212-730-1030
www.tinseltrading.com

Jenkins Woodworking
503-873-1246
www.jenkinswoodworking.com

Clover USA
800-233-1703
www.clover-usa.com

Coats and Clark
800-648-1479
www.coatsandclark.com

CANADA AND THE U.K.
YARNS

Diamond Yarn of Canada, Ltd.
416-736-6111
www.diamondyarn.com

Designer Yarns, Ltd.
www.designeryarns.uk.com

NOTIONS AND TOOLS

Creative Beadcraft
+44 (0) 1535 664222
www.creativebeadcraft.co.uk

Woolworks
www.woolworks.org/stores/england

SUGGESTED READING

Keim, Cecily and Kim Werker
Teach Yourself Visually: Crochet
Wiley Publishing, Inc., 2005
www.wiley.com

Okey, Shannon
Crochet Style
Creative Homeowner, 2007
www.creativehomeowner.com

Swenson, Amy
Not Your Mama's Felting
Wiley Publishing, Inc., 2007
www.wiley.com

Acknowledgments

Thank you to Stina Ramos, designer of all of the projects featured in *The Color Book of Felted Crochet*. Without Stina this book would simply be a collection of essays, not a beautiful book of fashionable felt creations. Stina has an amazing eye for design and color; she created beautiful garments that you'll want to make, too.

Thank you to Carole Buschmann, my aunt and first art teacher, for her early and continuing inspiration and guidance, and for her thoughtful and eloquent essay on color featured on pages 8 to 11.

Thank you to the yarn companies that donated their gorgeous fibers, including Be Sweet, Berroco, Blue Sky Alpacas, Brown Sheep Company, Cascade Yarns, Classic Elite Yarns, Malabrigo, and Vermont Organics; and to the manufacturers who loaned the beautiful garments and accessories featured with the felted items, especially Boden, Jane Bolinger, Rachel Reinhardt, Wendy Mink, Etienne Aigner, and Susana Monaco, Cable and Gauge, Urban Outfitters, Nanette Lepore, Benetton, Franco Sarto, and Carlos, Julie Sandlau, Suzy Roher, Reiss, Bettye Mueller, Steven, Parameter, Gabriella Zanzani, Spense, Alexis Hudson, and Beverly Feldman.

Thank you to Kim Werker who published my first pattern in the online magazine *Crochet Me* and who continues to inspire me with her editorial savvy and verve; to writer and designer, Shannon Okey for her friendship and helpful answers to my little "emergencies"; to senior editor, Carol Sterbenz for her amazing work, for her level head and grace under pressure, as well as her kindness and support, which made it a pleasure for me to be a part of this project; and to editorial assistant, Nora Grace, who supported everyone in the course of the project. Special thanks to photographers Damian Sandone and Steven Mays; Genevieve A. Sterbenz, producer; Deirdre Wegner, fashion stylist; and models Britney, Shelly, Carla, Whitney, Quimby, Sabrina, and Toni (APM); Alexandra and Cameron (ID Models); and Genevie (JG Models).

Though she's no longer here to receive thanks, I'm grateful to Helen Markos Buschmann, my "Sitto" and maternal grandmother, who taught me to crochet when I was eight years old. Thank you to Jean H. O'Neill, my paternal grandmother, who at 91 is still an accomplished practitioner of many crafts and has served as a muse for many of my projects; to my dad, John H. O'Neill, for his constant guidance and inspiration to me as a writer; to my brother John Markos O'Neill, who's always there to read my work and suggest clever titles; to my mom, Mary B. O'Neill, who is just as supportive and proud today as when I was a kid; to my children James "Jay" O'Neill Houck and Selma Jesse Houck for their patience; and to my husband, James P. Houck, for his relentless faith, support, and love.

Stina would like to add her thanks to author Amy O'Neill Houck "for her help with and ideas for the designs in the book, and for her patience. I couldn't have done it without her"; to crocheter Joyce Lemke for her help crocheting "Delicata"; and to crocheter Trudy Cullen for her help crocheting "Clematis."

Index

If you like **Color Book of Felted Crochet,**
take a look at other crochet titles in our line of Home Arts books.

Crochet Style: Chic and Sexy Accessories includes 27 of the most "now," one-of-a-kind accessories in a collection that features fabulously chic items.
- Gorgeous projects include a shrug, mod cap, cropped jacket, handbags, and other accessories
- Over 170 full-color fashion photographs
- A minicourse in crochet basics—from the tools to the essential techniques that build skills and confidence
- A concealed, spiral-bound book that allows "hands free" access to all of the information

Crochet Style
ISBN: 978-1-58011-331-1
CH Book # 265188
128 pages, 7¾" x 10⅞"
$19.95 US / $24.95 CAN

Complete Crochet
ISBN: 978-1-58011-294-9
CH Book # 265170
176 pages, 8½" x 10⅞"
$24.95 US / $32.95 CAN

Complete Crochet is an inspirational collection of over 25 stunning garments, accessories, home accents, and darling toys for babies and children.
- Over 150 color photographs, diagrams, and stitch details
- For beginner and veteran crocheters alike
- A comprehensive course in all of the crochet basics, including techniques and tools that build confidence to create original designs.
- Includes an expansive Stitch Library, practical advice for correcting mistakes, a glossary, and great sources for finding crochet tools and supplies

Party Crochet is a fun and stylish collection of fashionable designs delivered straight from the catwalk.
- Over 120 original full-color photographs accompanied by directions for all of the decorative techniques that are suited to all skill levels, including the beginner
- 24 amazing designs using glitzy metallic yarns, textured wools, and beads
- Ponchos, shrugs, shawls, cocktail dresses and bags, and a host of accessories to get you noticed
- Simple crochet instructions, along with essential advice on yarns, hooks, and basic techniques

Party Crochet
ISBN: 978-1-58011-330-4
CH Book # 265181
128 pages, 8½" x 10⅞"
$19.95 US / $25.95 CAN

So Simple Crochet
ISBN: 978-1-58011-276-5
CH Book # 265129
128 pages, 8¼" x 10⅞"
$19.95 US / $27.95 CAN

So Simple Crochet presents 24 original designs for beautiful and sophisticated separates.
- Over 110 full-color photographs, diagrams, and stitch charts
- Beginner-friendly techniques that yield professional-looking results with high style
- Projects ranging from trend-setting ponchos and scarves to gorgeous cardigans and cool mini-capes, jackets, and hats—many using today's most popular yarns
- Easy to follow, concise step-by-step directions
- Provides hours of fun and great-looking wardrobe pieces that have timeless appeal

Look for these and other fine books from **Creative Homeowner** books wherever books are sold.
For more information and to order direct, go to **www.creativehomeowner.com**